Accession no.
01136194

Inter te⊗t

The Language of Comics

'The book's practical strength is its blend of the academic and the accessible. It provides a fresh way of encouraging AS and A2 students to work with texts in a more analytical manner.'

Nicola Onyett, *Queen Margaret's School, York*

The INTERTEXT series has been specifically designed to meet the needs of contemporary English Language Studies. *Working with Texts: A core introduction to language analysis* (second edition, 2001) is the foundation text, which is complemented by a range of 'satellite' titles. These provide students with hands-on practical experience of textual analysis through special topics, and can be used individually or in conjunction with *Working with Texts*.

The Language of Comics:

◎ includes a large number of real comics, from individual frames to full comic strips;

◎ sets the analysis of comics within their historical context;

◎ explores various aspects of comics relevant to other types of text: the interaction between the verbal and the visual, the cohesive structure of texts, the ways speech and thought are reported, and points-of-view shifts in narrative;

◎ makes the case for comics as multi-modal texts and considers future developments in the genre;

◎ is user-friendly and accessible, and provides a full glossary.

Mario Saraceni is Lecturer at Assumption University, Bangkok, Thailand.

D1634389

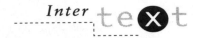

The Intertext series

◎ Why does the phrase 'spinning a yarn' refer both to using language and making cloth?

◎ What might a piece of literary writing have in common with an advert or a note from the milkman?

◎ Which aspects of language are important to understand when analysing texts?

The Routledge INTERTEXT series aims to develop readers' understanding of how texts work. It does this by showing some of the designs and patterns in the language from which they are made, by placing texts within the contexts in which they occur, and by exploring relationships between them.

The series consists of a foundation text, *Working with Texts: A core introduction to language analysis*, which looks at language aspects essential for the analysis of texts, and a range of satellite texts. These apply aspects of language to a particular topic area in more detail. They complement the core text and can also be used alone, providing the user has the foundation skills furnished by the core text.

Benefits of using this series:

◎ **Multi-disciplinary** – provides a foundation for the analysis of texts, supporting students who want to achieve a detailed focus on language.

◎ **Accessible** – no previous knowledge of language analysis is assumed, just an interest in language use.

◎ **Student-friendly** – contains activities relating to texts studied, commentaries after activities, highlighted key terms, suggestions for further reading and an index of terms.

◎ **Interactive** – offers a range of task-based activities for both class use and self-study.

◎ **Tried and tested** – written by a team of respected teachers and practitioners whose ideas and activities have been trialled independently.

The series editors:

Adrian Beard was until recently Head of English at Gosforth High School, and now works at the University of Newcastle upon Tyne. He is a Chief Examiner for AS- and A-level English Literature. He has written and lectured extensively on the subjects of literature and language. His publications include *Texts and Contexts* (Routledge).

Angela Goddard is Senior Lecturer in Language at the Centre for Human Communication, Manchester Metropolitan University, and is Chair of Examiners for A-level English Language. Her publications include *Researching Language* (second edition, Heinemann, 2000).

Core textbook:

Working with Texts: A core introduction to language analysis
(second edition, 2001)
Ronald Carter, Angela Goddard, Danuta Reah, Keith Sanger and Maggie Bowring

Satellite titles:

Language and Gender
Angela Goddard and Lindsey Meân Patterson

The Language of Advertising: Written texts
(second edition, 2002)
Angela Goddard

The Language of Children
Julia Gillen

The Language of Conversation
Francesca Pridham

The Language of Drama
Keith Sanger

The Language of Fiction
Keith Sanger

The Language of Humour
Alison Ross

The Language of ICT: Information and communication technology
Tim Shortis

The Language of Magazines
Linda McLoughlin

The Language of Newspapers
(second edition, 2002)
Danuta Reah

The Language of Poetry
John McRae

The Language of Politics
Adrian Beard

The Language of Speech and Writing
Sandra Cornbleet and Ronald Carter

The Language of Sport
Adrian Beard

The Language of Television
Jill Marshall and Angela Werndly

The Language
of Comics

© Mario Saraceni

·1651973   3wk

CHESTER COLLEGE

ACC. No.
01136194   DEPT. pd

CLASS No.
741·509 SAR

WARRINGTON LIBRARY
8/3/05

Routledge
Taylor & Francis Group

LONDON AND NEW YORK

First published 2003
by Routledge
11 New Fetter Lane, London EC4P 4EE

Simultaneously published in the USA and Canada
by Routledge
29 West 35th Street, New York, NY 10001

Routledge is an imprint of the Taylor & Francis Group

© 2003 Mario Saraceni

Typeset in Stone Sans/Stone Serif by
Florence Production Ltd, Stoodleigh, Devon
Printed and bound in Great Britain by
TJ International Ltd, Padstow, Cornwall

All rights reserved. No part of this book may be reprinted or
reproduced or utilised in any form or by any electronic,
mechanical, or other means, now known or hereafter invented,
including photocopying and recording, or in any information
storage or retrieval system, without permission in writing
from the publishers.

British Library Cataloguing in Publication Data
A catalogue record for this book is available from the British Library

Library of Congress Cataloging in Publication Data
Saraceni, Mario, 1969–
    The language of comics/Mario Saraceni.
       p. cm. – (Intertext)
    Includes bibliographical references and index.
    1. Comic books, strips, etc. – History and criticism.   I. Title.
    II. Intertext (London, England)
    PN6714.S27 2003
    741.5'09 – dc21   2002037048

ISBN 0–415–28670–0 (hbk)
ISBN 0–415–21422–X (pbk)

contents

acknowledgements

The author and publishers wish to thank the following for permission to reprint copyright material:

Eddie Campbell (Eddie Campbell Comics): illustrations from *Alec: The King Canute Crowd* (Figures 1.4, 4.5) and *From Hell* (Figure 2.8a)

Daniel Clowes (Fantagraphics): illustration from *Ghost World* (Figure 2.5)

Tom Hart: illustration from *The Sands* (Figure 3.4)

Dylan Horrocks: illustrations from *Hicksville* (Figures 1.1, 2.11, 5.1, 5.7)

N. Kanan (NBM): illustrations from *Lost Girl* (Figure 5.6)

Peter Kuper: illustrations from *Eye of the Beholder* (Figures 3.1, 3.7b) and *The System* (Figures 3.2, 3.3)

Jason Lutes: illustrations from *Jar of Fools* (Figures 1.2, 1.3, 5.8)

Matt Madden: illustrations from *Exercises in Style* (Figures 5.2, 5.3) and 'Roses are Red' (Figure 5.4c)

Peter Schrank (*The Economist*): Figure 2.4

Seth (Drawn and Quarterly): illustrations from *It's a Good Life If You Don't Weaken* (Figure 3.6)

Osamu Tezuka (Viz Comics): illustrations from *Adolf: An Exile in Japan* (Figure 4.2) and *Adolf: A Tale of the Twentieth Century* (Figure 4.4)

Adrian Tomine (Drawn and Quarterly): illustrations from *Sleepwalk* (Figures 1.5, 3.7a, 4.1, 5.4b) and *32 Stories* (Figures 2.6, 2.13, 2.14, 2.15)

Rich Tommaso (Fantagraphics): illustrations from *Clover Honey* (Figures 3.5, 4.3)

Joan Walsh: illustration from *My Busy Day*, Simon & Schuster, 1999 (Figure 2.12)

Andi Watson (ONI Press): illustrations from *Breakfast After Noon* (panels in Figure 2.10)

Every effort has been made to contact copyright holders. Any omissions brought to the attention of the publishers will be rectified in future editions.

What are comics?

The aim of Unit one is to explain what comics are and to provide a historical overview of their development, from the end of the nineteenth century to the present.

We think of comics as very modern texts, but it is possible to see connections between them and the communication systems of early civilisations. For example, the Egyptians used combinations of images and hieroglyphics, while narratives composed of sequences of pictures were common in other ancient cultures.

However, comics in the form we know now were first created in the last half of the nineteenth century in England. The first regular comic strip appeared in 1884 and featured the first comics hero, Ally Sloper. A few years later, in 1890, *Comic Cuts* appeared, which many consider to be the world's first regularly appearing comic.

1

American comics historians generally cite The Yellow Kid as the first comics character, which first appeared in 1896 in the Sunday edition of *The New York World*.

Thanks to their immediate success, comic strips soon became a regular feature of daily newspapers. Some of the characters created during this early period (Krazy Kat above all) have remained famous to this day.

Encouraged by their increasing popularity, in the early 1930s some publishers began to collect newspaper comic strips into books, hence the term 'comic book'. Such collections soon gained considerable success, while newspaper comic strips continued to be produced and other famous characters created, like Tarzan, Mickey Mouse and Dick Tracy.

The first comic book that had new material rather than reprints of newspaper strips was *New Fun Comics*, published in 1935. After this, many other publications followed, including the *Mickey Mouse Magazine* and *King Comics*, which contained famous characters like Popeye, Flash Gordon and Mandrake the Magician.

In the meantime, in Europe (especially in Belgium, France, Italy and Spain) children's magazines began to host comics as well. The popularity of comics rose steadily and many characters were created, the most famous of whom was Hergé's Tintin.

The first costumed hero was The Phantom, which appeared in *Ace Comics* in 1938. In June of the same year, Superman, the most famous superhero, made his debut in the first issue of *Action Comics*. Another famous superhero, Batman, first appeared the following year in *Detective Comics*. After the success of these three costumed heroes, many more were created in the same period, all with similar characteristics.

Will Eisner's The Spirit, created in 1940, was somewhat different, because of his sense of humour, for the fact that he did not wear the customary tights and, perhaps more importantly, because his stories were oriented to a more mature audience.

Towards the end of the 1940s the popularity of the superhero genre began to fade, while the so-called 'crime' and 'horror' comics gained more and more favour with comics readers. As crime and violence were increasingly featured in comics, many people began to worry about the effect that such publications might have on young readers. The most important figures in the expression of those worries were Doctor Frederic Wertham in America and George Pumphrey in Britain. The concerns over the presumed harmful influence of comics on children gave rise to campaigns against comics both in America and in Britain, which led to censure in the mid-1950s.

Perhaps it is not a coincidence that *Peanuts*, one of the most famous strips ever, was created during that period. Indeed, what was slowly happening was that comics were becoming more intellectual.

In the early 1960s there was a revival of the superhero genre, with the most popular new characters being Spider Man and The Fantastic Four. In the same period, even more important was the birth of underground comics, generally referred to as 'comix'. In these publications both content and form were more experimental and, above all, they were intended for adult readers. This trend grew towards the end of the 1960s and continued throughout the 1970s.

That comics became more intellectual was even more evident in Europe, where they began to attract serious scholarly attention. The number of adult-oriented publications grew and some of them were accredited with high artistic value, like Hugo Pratt's *Corto Maltese*.

In America, in the meantime, *A Contract with God*, written and drawn by Will Eisner at the end of the 1970s, was the first 'graphic novel' to be published. Although the term was later used mainly for commercial purposes, it reinforced the idea that comics were no longer only for children.

At the beginning of the 1980s, the *Manga* (the Japanese word for 'comics'), was introduced to the Western world, accompanied by an influx of Japanese animated cartoons to Europe and America. Osamu Tezuka is perhaps the most celebrated Japanese comics author.

The single title that definitely established comics as a proper adult art form was *Maus* (published between 1985 and 1992) by Art Spiegelman. This book, in which the author narrates his father's experience in the Nazi concentration camp of Auschwitz, gained international recognition and attracted the attention of a great number of critics, scholars and readers alike.

In the 1990s many so-called 'adult comics' were published, where serious themes were often accompanied by experimentation in the form. This trend continues today, with new authors exploring new possibilities provided by digital graphics and the Internet.

HOW COMIC ARE COMICS?

The word 'comics' can be very misleading about the nature of many of the publications that carry this label. It is certainly difficult to imagine any meaningful connection between such a term and, for example, a book like Art Spiegelman's *Maus*, which deals with the horrors of the Holocaust, or Joe Sacco's *Palestine*, which is about the problems of the Palestinian people. These are just two examples, but many more could be mentioned whose themes are hardly comical at all. In fact, even in the superhero comics, probably the most common type, there is little trace of comical elements. So, why are comics called 'comics'? The reason is the fact that the early strips, both in England and in America, were of a humorous nature (in America they were also called 'the funnies') and so the attribute 'comic' remained attached to this art form even when various new genres were developed later on.

In an attempt to create a term which would better describe the art form of comics, towards the end of the 1970s a new expression, 'graphic novel', was coined, to replace 'comic book'. However, the replacement never really occurred, while the term 'graphic novel' has been adopted mainly for commercial reasons. In fact, the distinction between 'comic books' and 'graphic novels' is nothing more than a matter of labels, and has barely anything to do with content or with any other feature.

Activity

Find out how comics have changed over the years. Ask older family members or friends which comics they read when they were your age. Show them some modern comics: how different are these? You can also easily get hold of old comics in second-hand book shops. Compare an old superhero comic book (e.g. *Superman*, *Spiderman* etc.) with a modern one or a 'recycled' version (e.g. *X Men*, *Spiderman*): what differences do you notice? Which ones are more comical? Which ones are more violent? Has the role of female characters changed? How about the language? And the graphics?

(Note: there is no commentary on this activity.)

THE COMPONENTS OF COMICS

The most important characteristics of comics are:

◎ employment of both words and pictures;

◎ texts organised into sequential units, graphically separated from each other.

Although the use of both words and pictures together, as such, is not a unique characteristic of comics, the way in which linguistic and pictorial elements interact with each other certainly is.

The arrangement into sequences of panels is the other fundamental characteristic of comics. This is what makes comics different from cartoons, which are composed of one panel only.

The language of comics has many similarities with the language we use every day. The components of our language are the words, and these are divided into **functional words** and **content words**. Functional words are those that are used to link other words together, like conjunctions (*and, but, or*), prepositions (*in, for, with*), articles (*the, a, an*) and so on. For example, in the sentence

James went to a concert with John and David

the words *to, a, with* and *and* are functional words because they have the *function* of linking the sentence together. The other words (*James, went, concert, John* and *David*) are content words, because they mean something, they have *content*. In every language there are many more content words than functional words. In English, for example, there are roughly half a million content words, but only about fifty functional words!

Something very similar happens in the language of comics, where there are *functional* components and *content* components. Look at the page of comics shown in Figure 1.1: which elements do you think are functional and which are content?

Figure 1.1

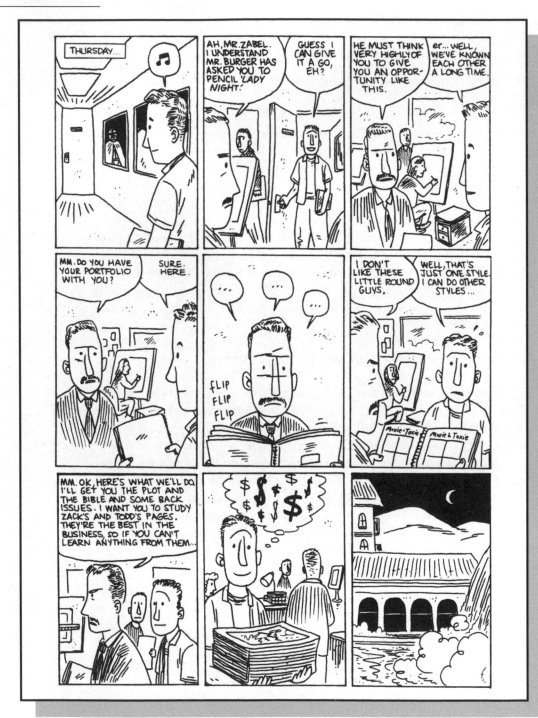

Commentary

Indicators of space or time, for example, are functional elements that are often used to connect different parts of the story together. An example is the caption in the first panel of Figure 1.1. Other functional elements on the same page are the musical notes (panel 1), representing the character's humming of a tune as he walks; the dots (panel 5), representing some unspoken reaction that the character must be feeling as he browses through the book; the sweat drops (panel 6), representing anxiety and nervousness; and the dollar signs (panel 8), representing the character's prediction of making a lot of money.

The sound effects in the fifth panel are particularly interesting. Notice how the sound *flip* is also an actual word in English. Indeed, the sound of this word resembles the noise produced by *flipping* through the pages of a book. There are many words like *flip* in English. These are called **onomatopoeic words**, and are words whose sounds are similar to the noises that the words refer to. Comics use this type of word very often: for example, *click*, *bang* and *gulp*.

Let's now look at the components of comics in more detail.

The panel

Each page is normally composed of six to nine rectangular frames called **panels**. Usually, panels display single instants of action or 'stills' and, although they are often referred to as 'frozen moments' and compared to photographs, their contents are actually much more varied. It is in fact very rare for a panel to represent only an instant of the story. That is because comics panels typically contain pieces of dialogue that are longer than the duration of a camera shot (i.e. a fraction of a second). For this reason they are perceived as different from photographs, for example. The reader of comics considers the panel as a portion – which can be of various lengths – of the narrative, where something actually takes place and takes time.

Dialogues are not the only elements indicating that the duration of panels goes beyond single instants. Panel 5 of Figure 1.1, for example, represents a *whole* event – a character flipping through the pages of a book – not just a point in time.

At other times the duration of panels is also represented by their width. In the short extract shown in Figure 1.2, the second panel is much wider than the others, while the third one is much narrower, which

7

reflects the different duration of the events shown: in the second panel a marble is thrown with force, its route indicated by a long motion line across the sky, while the following panel shows the precise moment in which the marble falls in the water with a splash.

Figure 1.2

Modifications of the panel border are sometimes used in order to convey the idea that the panel portrays the memory or the dream of a character, as shown in the first two panels of Figure 1.3.

Figure 1.3

The gutter

Each panel is separated from the others by a blank space called the **gutter**. The gutter is a very important element, since it is the space containing all that happens between the panels. This means that the reader has to guess the missing elements in order to reconstruct the flow of the story. The gutter is similar to the space that divides one sentence from the next: there is always a certain amount of information that is missing from the narrative and the readers have to provide it for themselves.

The actual width of the gutter is not very important; what counts is the division itself between the panels. Some authors of comics, for example, prefer to draw panels adjacent to one another, with no blank space between them; but this is only a stylistic choice, as the separation remains there, as does the concept of the gutter. Such comics are sometimes referred to as 'gutterless'. However, this is misleading, because it only takes into account the physical space, rather than the conceptual separation, between panels.

The balloon

The balloon is probably the element that most people associate with comics. It is the space in which most of the verbal text is contained. Balloons are used to report speech or thought, and that is why the terms **speech balloon** and **thought balloon** are used.

Typically, balloons are of oval or cloud-like shape, but variations are possible and sometimes significant. In the case of adaptations of classics of literature, for example, the shape of the balloons is often square – this unusual shape is used in order to give more respectability to the publication.

The tail of the balloon indicates the character who is speaking (or thinking). Normally the tail looks like a small pointed projection, but it can sometimes be a simple line. An important variation is when the tail is formed of a series of small bubbles, which indicate that the balloon is a thought balloon (panel 8 in Figure 1.1). The function of the tail is equivalent to that of clauses like 'he said' or 'Ann thought' in reported speech or thought.

The caption

The caption is the other element of comics that contains linguistic elements. Unlike the balloon, the caption is not positioned inside the panel, but is always a separate entity, often on the top of the panel, but sometimes at the bottom or on the left side. Normally the text contained in the caption represents the narrator's voice, very similar to the background voice that is sometimes heard in films. Its function is to add information to the dialogues contained in the rest of the panel.

In its simplest form, a caption is just an indicator of space and/or time (panel 1 in Figure 1.1 on p. 6).

In other cases the caption has the function of providing information to help the reader reconstruct the flow between panels, filling the gap represented by the gutter (Figure 1.4).

Figure 1.4

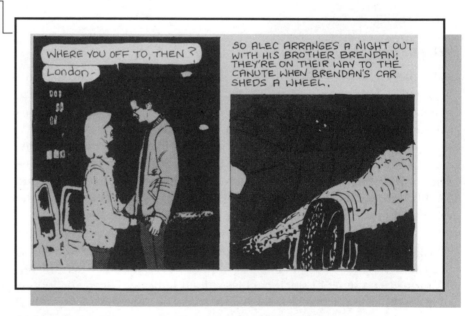

Sometimes captions have a fundamental importance in the narration of the story, since they contain most or all of the linguistic components of the text (Figure 1.5).

Figure 1.5

Activity

Collect various types of comics (children's comics, adult comics, old comics, modern comics etc.) and analyse the elements that compose them:

◎   What is the shape and the size of the panels?

◎   How are speech and thought balloons represented?

◎   Are there any captions? How do they help you follow the story?

◎   how easy is it for you to find the connection between each panel and the next?

(Note: there is no commentary on this activity.)

SUMMARY

This unit has provided an historical overview of comics, from their first appearance in newspapers to modern 'adult' comics. The main components of comics have also been described, so that you now have sufficient information to help you through the other units in the book.

Words and pictures

The aim of Unit two is to illustrate the ways in which words and pictures interact in comics as well as in other media.

In Unit one you read that one of the main characteristics of comics is the fact that they employ both words and pictures at the same time. In this unit you are going to learn more about the ways in which these two elements interact with one another.

In fact, words and pictures exist side by side not only in comics, but also in other media and types of texts: advertisements, newspapers, the Internet, children's books, TV and film all use a mix of verbal and visual elements. So, much of what is covered in this unit also applies to these other media.

What relationships exist between words and pictures? Basically these are of two kinds:

◎   a blend

◎   a collaboration.

THE BLEND BETWEEN WORDS AND PICTURES

It is normally thought that words and pictures are very different from each other. But this is not always the case. Think about it: when words are printed or written, in order to read them you have to *look* at them. This means that, besides being a verbal entity, a word on paper is also a *visual* entity. It might be the case, then, that the way we understand the meaning of words may also depend on the way words look.

At the same time, there are many pictures that can mean something fairly precise across a number of different cultures. Take the sign in Figure 2.1, for example: the way you immediately associate a meaning with this symbol is very similar to the way you do the same thing with actual words. It is a special kind of reading: could we say that pictures can be *read*?

Figure 2.1

To understand these concepts better, it will be useful to consider for a moment the discipline of **semiotics**, which studies human and non-human communication.

SEMIOTICS AND THE IDEA OF THE SIGN

At the basis of semiotics is the idea of **sign**. A sign is something that *stands* for something else. Essentially, it is anything capable of meaning. There are three main types of signs:

- An **icon** resembles what it means. Most pictures are icons, because they are similar to what they represent. So, a picture of a dog stands for that dog because it resembles it.

- An **index** indicates the presence of something else. Smoke, for example, is an index of fire. Smoke stands for fire, because it indicates its presence.

- A **symbol** is associated to its meaning by virtue of a shared convention. Words are typical examples of symbols. The sequence of letters 'd-o-g' stands for the idea of 'dog' not because it resembles a dog but because that is its conventional meaning in the English language. In these cases we also talk about arbitrary meaning.

In this unit we will concentrate only on icons and symbols. At this point we can say that pictures tend to be iconic and words tend to be symbolic. So, we can represent the opposition between words and pictures by means of a simple diagram:

symbols   icons

(words)   (pictures)

Activity

Out of the list of road signs in Figure 2.2, which ones do you think are iconic and which ones symbolic? Why? Are you always sure of your choices?

Figure 2.2

Road signs are useful for understanding the difference between symbol and icon. For many of them it is fairly easy to recognise the pictures shown. This is the case for signs (a), (b), (d) and (f), since in all of them the pictures *resemble* what they mean: rocks falling from a cliff, a man walking, a man working and a bicycle. By contrast, signs (c) and (e) don't resemble anything and their meanings are entirely based on some shared convention. Drivers need to know that a sign with a white horizontal bar in the middle of a red circle means 'no entry', and that a sign with one or two diagonal red bars in a blue circle means 'no parking'. There is no way they can guess the meanings of these signs.

This distinction, however, doesn't necessarily mean that the iconic road signs are not symbolic as well, at least to a certain degree. The picture of a bicycle alone, for example, is not enough to convey the meaning of sign (f) ('no cycling'). The colour of the sign plays an important role. The sign in Figure 2.3, for example, has the opposite meaning of (f), and such a difference is not based on resemblance, but on shared convention.

Figure 2.3

LOOKING AT WORDS

Although the symbols and icons diagram (see p. 15) represents an opposition between symbols and icons, there isn't necessarily a clear-cut difference. Instead of being purely iconic or purely symbolic, many signs can be placed along a scale *between* symbol and icon. Look, for example, at the symbol in Figure 2.1. Its meaning is conventionally established worldwide. But is it completely arbitrary? Although the resemblance is certainly not very faithful, the shapes of the two figures do remind us of what they represent. So, if we were to place Figure 2.1 along the symbol/icon scale, where would we put it? The exact point doesn't matter, but what is important is that it would probably *not* be on either end of the scale, but somewhere between the two ends. So we could say that this figure is symbolic *and* iconic at the same time.

The same can apply to words, too. If you take any printed text you are bound to find a number of cases where the shapes and sizes of words add some information to their literal meaning. Consider the pages of this book: bigger words are used for chapter titles, while bold typeface is used for section headings and for glossed terms. This already indicates that the look of words does contribute something to their meaning. Italics, for example, are also used in order to *emphasise* certain words. Compare, for example, the following sentences:

I need to tell you something.

I *need* to tell you something.

I need to *tell* you something.

I need to tell *you* something.

I need to tell you *something*.

Each sentence is composed of exactly the same words, but each one of them looks different from the others. Do they have exactly the same meaning?

The relationship between the look of words and their meaning can be more sophisticated. Consider the cartoon in Figure 2.4. Is it a word or a picture? In fact it is both. The visual and the verbal aspects support each other in conveying the meaning of the cartoon. The same effect wouldn't be achieved if the word 'democracy' were simply typed, or if the system of pipes didn't form the letters 'd-e-m-o-c-r-a-c-y'. Where would we place this word/picture along the symbol/icon scale? Probably right in the middle!

Figure 2.4

Activity

Collect the following texts: the opening page of a novel, the front page of a broadsheet newspaper, the front page of a tabloid newspaper, a train or bus timetable leaflet and the homepage of your school/college/university web site. How does each text exploit the visual aspect of words? Which text makes the most use of it? How does the visual aspect of words contribute to their meaning? Could the texts be rewritten using no visual features at all?

(Note: there is no commentary on this activity.)

THE VISUAL ASPECT OF WORDS IN COMICS

In comics the visual aspect of words has great significance. Bold type is normally used to emphasise certain words or to indicate loudness. In the panel in Figure 2.5 the two friends Enid and Rebecca are watching TV and they scream in horror when they see someone who has, according to them, awful hair. All the bold words in the two girls' speech balloons represent shouting, while the bold 'count' in the speech balloon from the TV indicates emphasis. Also notice the size of the letters in the scream 'aieeee': in comics, enlarged letters are very commonly used in order to convey loud speech or noises.

Figure 2.5

In comics the graphical value of words can be exploited because letters are not usually typed, but handwritten. Handwriting can be considered a special kind of drawing and it allows the artist much more freedom than a set typeface. Figure 2.6 is an example of *drawn* words, where the resulting image is neither purely verbal nor purely visual, but a blend of the two, and the meaning is based on both aspects. The expression of pain conveyed is particularly effective. Mood can also be represented in interesting ways.

Figure 2.6

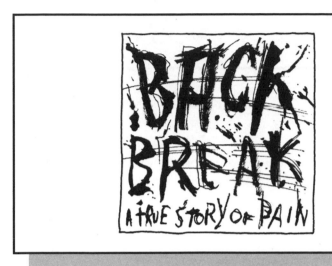

Handwriting is particularly good for the representation of mood and feeling, not only because it allows greater creativity in the style, but also because it is more closely associated with the characters than a mechanical typeface would be. This is because we tend to associate handwriting with human agency. The irregular shapes of the letters resemble the irregular patterns in the way people speak, with varying tones and loudness of voice. Rigidly uniform writing, on the other hand, would *sound* unnatural and almost robot-like. Compare, for example, the two balloons in Figure 2.7: which one seems more natural?

Figure 2.7

So, in the symbol/icon scale, the position of the kind of writing found in comics can be variable, because it is very often a *blend* of symbolic and iconic characteristics.

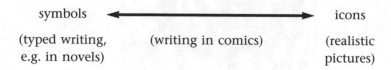

symbols ←——————————————————→ icons

(typed writing, (writing in comics) (realistic
e.g. in novels)   pictures)

This means that in comics (and in other media) words can be looked at as well as read. Their meanings derive from their visual as well as from their verbal value.

Let's shift our focus to pictures now. Pictures are normally looked at – can they also be *read*?

READING PICTURES

So far we have defined pictures as iconic entities, that is, signs which mean what they mean because of resemblance. But we have also said that between symbols and icons there isn't a very distinct difference. So the question is: can pictures be symbolic and therefore similar to words? Since symbols are signs whose meanings are arbitrarily assigned by convention, the question of whether or not pictures can be symbolic can be reformulated as: to what extent does the meaning of a given picture depend on convention?

Very realistic pictures, like photographs for example, are easily associated with the subjects they represent. Their degree of resemblance is very high. However, things are different when pictures become more stylised and less realistic. Consider for example the two pictures in Figure 2.8. The one at the top (a) is a drawing of St Paul's Cathedral in London and the one below (b) is a photograph of the same subject. Although it is a fairly realistic one, the drawing only uses black and white, and makes use of certain conventional devices to render the shaded parts of the building. Compared to the photograph, the recognition of the subject represented relies more on a certain amount of shared convention.

Figure 2.8

(a)

(b)

Now look at Figure 2.9. Here, you would probably still recognise that the subject is a church. But how much of that recognition is due to convention and how much is it due to actual resemblance? The picture is, after all, composed only of ten straight lines. It is largely by convention that we identify a roof, two walls, a tower and a cross. Besides, the cross itself is a symbol of Christianity. So, if we were to place these three pictures along our symbol/icon scale, we would probably have a different position for each one of them:

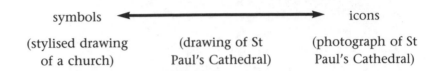

symbols		icons
(stylised drawing of a church)	(drawing of St Paul's Cathedral)	(photograph of St Paul's Cathedral)

Figure 2.9

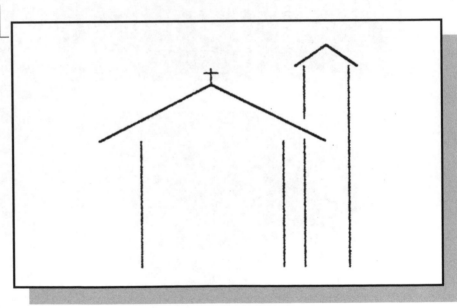

So, similarly to what we have seen for words, pictures can be characterised by a blend of symbolic and iconic features. Once again, this blend is particularly prominent in comics.

PICTURES IN COMICS

The drawing in Figure 2.8(a) is taken from a graphic novel. We have already seen how it is more stylised than a photograph. Although there may be considerable variations among different genres and different authors, in comics pictures are indeed generally rather stylised. This stylisation places the pictorial elements of comics relatively closer to the symbol end of the scale and therefore closer to linguistic elements.

Repetitive images and recognisable symbols are used very commonly in comics and form their pictorial vocabulary. Faces and facial expressions demonstrate well the use of such special vocabulary. In Figure 2.10 you can see a series of different facial expressions. Notice how the key elements are the eyebrows and the mouth, which are represented by simple straight or curved lines. These lines have a symbolic value as they are repeated over and over again in comics to convey the same meaning, much in the way words do. In this sense, we could say that in such cases we look at pictures but we also *read* them.

Figure 2.10

Where could we place the faces of Figure 2.10 along our symbol/icon scale? Again, it's difficult to determine a precise position, but we know that they exhibit both iconic and symbolic characteristics, so it is likely that an appropriate location would be towards the middle of the scale.

Pictures in comics can be even more symbolic than the ones we've seen so far. A variety of symbols are commonly used, which stand for specific mental states. Some of them are shown in Figure 2.11: small stars represent pain; zigzagged lines over a character's head mean anger; bubbles represent drunkenness or confusion; sweat drops mean great surprise or anxiety, and so on. The meanings of all these pictures are highly symbolic, while their *iconicity* can hardly be said to be there. How do stars resemble the feeling of pain? So this is a step closer towards the symbol end of the scale.

Figure 2.11

So, pictures, like words, can be iconic and symbolic to various degrees. What happens if we put words *and* pictures on the symbol/icon scale at the same time?

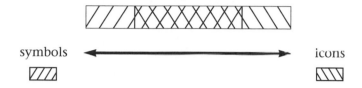

symbols ⟵⟶ icons

What happens is that the areas covered by words and pictures partially overlap. The actual amount of overlap varies according to the style of each individual author, especially because some comics artists do not exploit the visuality of writing as much as others, but what is important is that in comics the overlap is always there. This overlap represents the blend between words and pictures, which is a major feature of the language of comics.

The *blend* between words and pictures refers, then, to instances where the verbal and the visual are merged together in the same sign, which is therefore both symbolic and iconic. If the blend of words and pictures forms the vocabulary of the language of comics, the collaboration between the two represents its grammar. Unlike the *blend*, the *collaboration* between words and pictures refers to cases where the two remain distinct from one another, but work together in order to convey meaning. The next section explores this in more detail.

THE COLLABORATION BETWEEN WORDS AND PICTURES

In order to best understand the way in which words and pictures collaborate in comics, it may be a good idea to see what kind of relationship exists between the two in children's books.

Children's books make extensive use of pictures, although, interestingly, they become fewer and more space is occupied by words as the age of the target reader increases. This is because the main function of pictures in children's books is to aid understanding. Look at Figure 2.12, for example. Here the picture clearly shows a child crawling and touching a flower, and that's exactly what the text below it says: 'Baby crawls and touches a flower.' Pictures, in cases like this, illustrate the words; they explain the meaning of words that are still a little unfamiliar to very young readers. To an adult reader the presence of both words and pictures seems redundant, since both mean the same thing.

Figure 2.12

Baby crawls
and touches a flower.

In comics, things are very different: words and pictures are far from being redundant. In comics, that is, words and pictures don't just mirror one another, but interact in many different ways, and each of the two contributes its own share for the interpretation of the text.

Activity

Read Text: Happy Anniversary, which is the verbal text of a story that was originally presented in comics format. Then look at the panels in Figures 2.13, 2.14 and 2.15, which will give you a sense of how the story was illustrated.

◎   What does the pictorial representation add to the verbal text?

◎   How do the verbal and visual elements interact?

Text: Happy Anniversary

– Hey, honey!
– Hi there. Happy anniversary. These are for you.
– Eeps! We said no presents! I didn't . . .
– Don't worry about it! Oh . . . this goes with it.
– Tsk! C'mon in.
[The card reads: *Jeannette, On the occasion of our third year together . . . looking forward to many more. I love you!*]
– Aw . . . Thanks, hon. I love it when you give me drawings!
– Eh . . . It's nothing big.
– But now I feel bad that I didn't get you anything.
– Hey . . . Forget it!
– Well, have a sit, mister. Dinner's just about ready.
– Hey, you sure you don't wanna go out to a fancy restaurant or something? It *is* a
     special occasion and all . . .
– Yes, I'm sure. I've made a very nice meal for us, okay?
[After dinner, still at the table]
– Really . . . I'm stuffed. That was absolutely delicious!
– Did everything taste okay to you?
– It beat any ol' restaurant in town.
– Well, the chicken was a little overcooked . . .
– Nah . . . It was perfect. Just the way I like it.
– Ha-ha . . . You're just easy to please.
[On the couch, watching TV]
– Hon, can I ask you something?
– Yeah, sure.
– Are you happy?
– What do you mean about that?
– I don't know . . . About me. With the relationship.
– Why? I mean, what's the matter?
– I don't know. I was just wondering.
– But *why*? What the *fuck* are you saying? If you're trying to say you wanna . . . break
     up, or . . .
– I don't know what I'm trying to say. Is that what *you* want?
– No . . . Not at all . . . Why would I want that? I love you . . . C'mon . . . Let's not wreck
     our anniversary.
– Okay, baby. I'm sorry.
[In bed]
– You know, I think a lot of times you don't say what's on your mind. You keep a lot
     inside. I just wanted to know. I mean, sometimes people stay together out of habit
     . . . or indifference . . . both of them afraid to say anything. Sometimes I just think
     maybe . . .
– Listen . . . You're about the most important thing in my life right now. I guess I should
     show it more. I don't know what I'd do if we ever . . . I'm sorry I got mad tonight,
     but you scared me.
– It's okay, I know.

Figure 2.13

Figure 2.14

Figure 2.15

Commentary

This story represents a very good example of the interaction between words and pictures in comics. The verbal text tells a fairly simple story of a young couple celebrating their anniversary. What can be understood from the verbal text is: in a relationship where everything is seemingly fine, the girl wonders whether the bliss is actual or only apparent, that is, whether her boyfriend is hiding unspoken discontent within himself; the boyfriend, on his part, reassures her that there are no problems. The girl's final statement, 'It's okay, I know', seems to confirm the boyfriend's words, bringing everything back to normality.

31

A number of words and expressions in the text contribute to conveying a sense of general positiveness and regularity: 'I love it', 'a very nice meal', 'absolutely delicious', 'it was perfect' and 'just the way I like it'. The card that the boyfriend gives the girl is a very conventional one. There are also a number of expressions aimed at reassuring, such as 'Don't worry about it', 'Hey, forget it' and 'Yes, I'm sure', as well as the final exchange between the two partners.

This is what the verbal text tells us. One characteristic of the drawings that seems to be important in the story is the presence of an abnormal quantity of straight lines. In Figure 2.13 you can see that straight lines are just about everywhere – on the furniture, on the window frame and on the characters' clothes. Notice especially those on the boyfriend's shirt: the checked patterns are so regular that the shirt looks unnaturally flat.

The visual aspect of the title (Figure 2.14) is also significant. The background is composed of two segments, one white one black, and the words are black on the white section, and white on the black section, again giving a sense of neatness and regularity.

The final page of the story is completely wordless. Figure 2.15 shows the last six panels, where the girl is waking up the next morning. The expression on her face doesn't seem happy. Again you can see straight lines, but in the fourth and fifth panel something important happens. She walks to the window and pulls down one of the strips of the Venetian blind with a finger to look outside. The Venetian blind is drawn as a series of straight parallel lines, so the girl's action bends a few of these lines. This would be a totally insignificant event in any other story, but here it acquires great importance. The bending of the strips in the Venetian blind represents a break in the mechanical regularity that pervades the relationship between the two characters. Also, this break allows the girl to gaze outside and this acquires an extra significance: all the straight lines inside can be seen as the bars of a cage in which she feels trapped.

This is of course a subjective interpretation, but what is significant is that it is only possible through the interaction of words and pictures. The verbal text alone doesn't tell the whole story – it needs collaboration from the visual text, which provides the reader with fundamental elements for interpretation.

SUMMARY

This unit has tried to explain the two types of relationship that exist between words and pictures in comics: blend and collaboration. We have seen how words can be used and perceived as images, and how certain pictures convey their meaning in a way which makes them similar to words. We have also seen how, even when they are clearly distinct entities, words and pictures interact with one another in an inseparable cooperation for the conveyance of meaning.

Unit three

Between the panels

This unit will cover the second main characteristic of the language of comics: the sequential organisation of panels.

This characteristic is what distinguishes comics from cartoons. The two media are similar in the way they make use of words and pictures, but they differ in the fact that cartoons are always composed of *only one panel*, whereas comics are always composed of *more than one panel*. Although the distinction may not seem very remarkable, this unit will explain precisely why the sequential nature of comics is so important.

CARTOONS, COMICS AND LANGUAGE

To begin to understand the important difference between cartoons and comics, think about language: normally people don't use isolated sentences but longer stretches of language (texts). It is very rare, although not impossible, to read or hear individual sentences by themselves. As you read this book, for example, you read one sentence after another in sequence. You make sense of each sentence based on the preceding ones and those that follow. Every sentence carries some information and, as you read on, you use that information to understand the sentences that follow. Sometimes you can't quite understand what a portion of text means until you read the next few sentences. At any given point, therefore, you rely on what is generally called the **textual context**, that is, the language that *surrounds* a portion of text.

Isolated sentences do exist, but they are exceptions, rather than the norm. 'Beware of the dog', 'no smoking' and similar notices do occur, of course. In order to understand them you can't rely on the textual context because there isn't any. In these cases you have to resort to the **extra-textual context**, your knowledge of the world. If you see a sign with the single sentence, 'Mrs Cobley's office is now on the third floor', you may understand the individual words, but in order to fully understand the sentence you need to refer to information you may already have, such as the building where you are, who Mrs Cobley is, how to get to the third floor, and to the information you are going to gain (where exactly her office is on the third floor).

Cartoons are like single sentences: in order to understand them you need to have some extra-textual information. The cartoon in Figure 2.4 in the previous unit, for example, can only be fully understood if one has knowledge of what it refers to (contemporary Russia). You may understand the individual components (the meaning of the word 'democracy' and of the system of pipes) but you will miss the point of the cartoon without that information.

The structure of comics, on the other hand, is similar to that of language texts: comics texts are formed of strings of panels in the same way as language texts are formed of strings of sentences.

The question is: how are the various panels of a comic connected to one another so as to form a unified whole?

COHESION

The aspect of text analysis that is concerned with the ways in which sentences are connected to one another is called **cohesion**. This word comes from the Latin *cohaesus*, which means 'cling together'. The concept of cohesion doesn't apply only to language texts, but to texts in general, including comics. In fact, because of their particular panel-based structure, it can be very interesting to analyse comics texts from the point of view of cohesion. So, how do panels cling together?

REPETITION

One fundamental way in which two or more panels are linked together is by having elements in common. These can be the same characters, objects, buildings, background, or even very small details.

Activity

Look at the group of panels in Figure 3.1 and decide which panels go together. How did you make your decisions?

Figure 3.1

Commentary

In this simple activity the first two panels are connected to each other by repetition. Of course repetition doesn't occur only between two panels. What normally happens is that each panel conveys some information, and part of that information is repeated in the next panel, which, in turn, will share some information with the panel after, and so on. In this way, chains of connected panels are formed. So, typically, each panel will have some information repeated from the previous one and, at the same time, add some new information. What is repeated is called **given information**, while what is added is called **new information**.

Activity

Look at the sequence of panels in Figure 3.2. How does given and new information help to link the panels together? Why do you think the author has chosen to link the panels in the way he did?

Figure 3.2

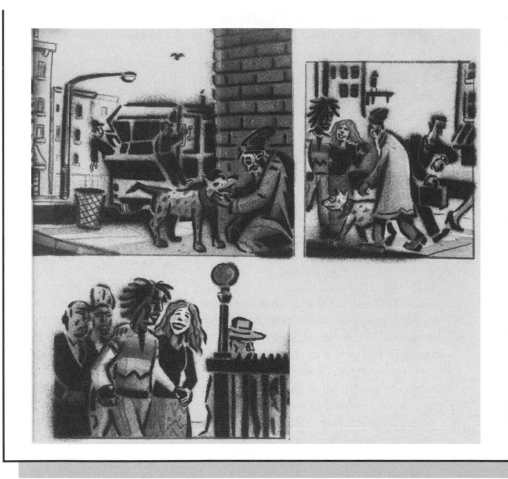

Commentary

In this sequence the connection of each panel to the next is based on one common element:

◎   the dove links the first panel to the second;

◎   the rubbish collectors link the second panel to the third;

◎   the homeless person and his dog link the third panel to the fourth;

◎   the young couple link the fourth panel to the fifth.

39

So, what happens is that the new element in one panel becomes the given element in the next. The panels are linked together according to the following structure:

panel 1:   given   –
           new   *the man at the window* and
                      the dove

panel 2:   given   *the dove*
           new   *the rubbish collectors*

panel 3:   given   *the rubbish collectors*
           new   *the homeless man and his dog*

panel 4:   given   *the homeless man and his dog*
           new   *the young couple*

panel 5:   given   *the young couple*
           new   –

This sequence is taken from a comic book (*The System* by Peter Kuper) in which the author makes extensive use of repetition as a way of linking panels together. The narrative, which depicts various aspects of modern life in New York, is arranged into short flashes linked together by a clever intersection of different stories, with different characters as protagonists. In fact the real story in *The System* is the system itself: everything that happens within the system somehow affects all those who are part of it. It is like a complex mechanism in which every element has a function, a role and a more or less direct influence over the other elements.

The sequence in Figure 3.2 has the function of introducing new characters to the reader. In this novel the introduction of new characters is always cleverly realised through sequences based on the relationship between given and new: what is new in one panel becomes given in the next. The author is thus able to introduce new characters in rapid succession and in an extremely economical way, while, at the same time, the given elements prevent the reader from being displaced.

Activity

In the previous activity you saw the role of a given–new structure in connecting panels together. Now look at the sequences in both parts of Figure 3.3. How are the panels linked to one another? How would you represent the links in a diagram, using given and new elements? How is this diagram different from the one that refers to Figure 3.2?

Figure 3.3a

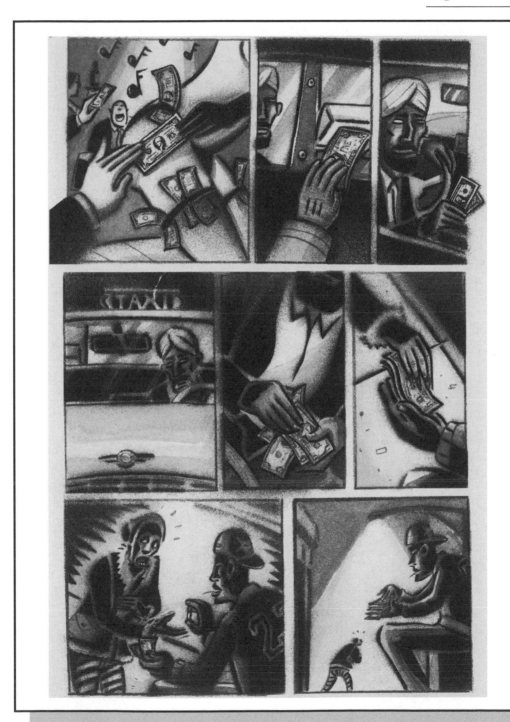

Figure 3.3b

Here the different scenes and characters are connected by one repeated element: money. The function of the continuous presence of money is not only to provide a connection for the sequence, but also to convey the idea that money is a pervasive aspect in all the components of 'the system'.

Notice how the content of the ninth panel 'merges' into the content of the tenth panel. In this particular case, the hands of the pusher merge into those of the policeman. This is a technique that Kuper uses frequently and involves the identification of two elements. In language, this is called **synonymy**, which is the use of two or more words with the same or similar meaning (see the core book of this series, *Working with Texts*). Kuper exploits it by putting together elements that are not normally associated with each other. Here, for example, the fact that the two pairs of hands are put in such close relation suggests that there is not much difference between the pusher and the policeman (as the development of the story reveals).

In the examples you have seen so far repetition occurs in adjacent panels, but one interesting aspect of repetition is the fact that it can also link panels that are apart from each other. In fact, repetition helps the reader perceive connections across the whole length of a text. There are graphic novels in which panels are connected to one another even though they are several pages apart. Thanks to the linking force of repetition, authors of comics can decide to connect panels together regardless of the distance between them. This means that sometimes there may be strings of panels that look totally disconnected from one another, simply because they are connected to other panels found somewhere else in the text.

Activity

Look at the series of panels in Figure 3.4. Does it seem cohesive? How different is it from the previous sequences? Can you understand what happens?

Figure 3.4

CHESTER COLLEGE WARRINGTON LIBRARY

Commentary

Figure 3.4 is not a random collection of four panels, but is in fact an extract from a graphic novel. The reason why it's difficult to see the connections between them is that each of the four panels is linked to other panels located elsewhere in the story. This confirms that the units that compose a text don't have to be linked together in linear sequences, as connections can exist between units that are located in different positions within the text.

Extension

Consider Figure 3.4 again and, individually or in small groups, devise a very short story based on those four panels. Then compare your story with that written by other groups and discuss the differences.

Commentary

This activity reveals another interesting aspect of the way in which the panels of a text hang together. Even though there is no repetition and there are no evident links, you probably still tried to understand what is happening in the four panels in Figure 3.4. In writing your short narrative you tried to reconstruct a story out of the fragments available.

Repetition, in its various forms, is a visible feature of the text but, at the same time, it is not a necessary or a sufficient condition for a string of panels/sentences to be perceived as a text. That's because, ultimately, texts are what readers *perceive* as texts. It is important to notice that, even in the absence of explicit links, readers will try to find possible ways in which a series of panels or sentences make sense together, as long as such a series is presented to them as a text.

The perception of series of panels or sentences as unified texts is called **coherence**.

COHERENCE

While cohesion is a property of the text itself, coherence has to do with the reader's interpretation. The next activity will give you a first idea of the difference between cohesion and coherence.

Activity

Consider the panels in Figure 3.1 on p. 37 again. You saw that repetition was a strong connecting feature. But see if you can find other types of links between the panels. Those 'other types of links' are all about the concept of coherence.

Commentary

If cohesion is largely based on repetition, what is coherence based on? It is not easy to answer this question, because in order to analyse the readers' interpretation one would need to have access to their minds! However, there are certain processes of the minds of human beings that seem to be similar for everyone. Two of these processes are:

◎   the capacity to recognise elements belonging to the same **semantic field** (area of meaning);

◎   **inference**, the capacity to make sense of incomplete information.

SEMANTIC FIELD

If you consider the words *station*, *train*, *platform*, *passengers* and *railway*, you probably feel that they are somehow connected. That's because you relate them to a common area of meaning, called a *semantic field* – in this case, probably that of 'railway station'. The word 'probably' has to be used here, because each individual may provide a different phrase, such as 'train journey' for example. Semantic fields are not fixed categories of words, but they have variable sizes and overlap with one another. The words listed above, for example, together with many others like *car*, *ticket*, *timetable*, *airport* and *taxi*, may belong to the broader semantic field of 'transportation'.

Activity

How are the panels in Figure 3.5 connected to one another? Can you identify a common semantic field? With which other semantic fields would you associate some of the panels?

Figure 3.5

Commentary

While in the previous texts the panels were linked together mainly by repetition, in this passage the binding force is of a different nature. The only instance of actual repetition occurs between the fifth and the seventh panels, while what really holds the sequence together are relations based on a common semantic field. Running horses, jockeys and spectators are all elements that belong to the same semantic field – the horse-racing track shown in the first panel.

It is important to remember that semantic fields are mental representations, not classes of words that share some objective common characteristics. The classic word-association game, where one person mentions one word and another person has to mention the first word that comes to mind, is based on the concept of semantic field. The fact that different people will associate words in different ways show that semantic fields are subjective rather than objective.

Everyone has a different knowledge of the world; each person's experience is different from anyone else's and so are the ways in which words are associated with one another.

Activity

What do the sequences in both parts of Figure 3.6 represent? What associations link the panels together? What does each panel mean by itself? Can you provide a title for the sequence?

Figure 3.6

Figure 3.6 *(cont.)*

Commentary

The first thing that can be noticed is that some of panels in Figure 3.6 are connected with weather conditions:

panel 1:   heat
panel 6:   rain
panel 11:   snow

The order of these particular panels, heat–rain–snow doesn't seem coincidental. In some parts of the world this sequence corresponds to the passing of seasons. Other panels show scenes that are normally associated with a particular period of the year, suggesting an overall 'story' of an annual cycle.

However, the recognition of this passage as a seasonal cycle is not necessarily so straightforward. The extract is taken from a graphic novel set in Canada. In many parts of the world the year is not divided into the same seasons as those represented here. In some regions there is never any snow, for example, or there are only two seasons, one dry and one rainy. In addition, some of the panels show scenes whose significance may not be readily understood by people who come from places other than that in which the text is set. The presence of panel 3, for example, can only be understood by people who come from areas where roadworks are only done in the summer. The scenes in panels 7, 8 and 9 are associated with autumn by readers who live in places where leaves fall and where Hallowe'en in celebrated in that period of the year. Similarly, the last three panels are only relevant to those familiar with ice hockey.

So, in order to make sense of the series of panels in Figure 3.6 readers need to have specific knowledge of the world and cultural background. In fact this is true for *any* text: readers react to texts in different ways because of their different backgrounds.

Coherence is not only in the text but also in the reader's mind. In fact, reading is something that involves what is *not* in the text as well as what is present. In every text some information is missing, and it's up to the reader to reconstruct the full story, to infer the missing pieces.

INFERENCE: BRIDGING THE GAPS

According to a very simple definition, a text is a collection of units – sentences or, in the case of comics, panels. This means that, between every unit and the next, there is an interruption, a white space, in which something is left out. Consider the following short extract:

I caught the 3 o'clock bus. It was very hot. I ate at Céleste's restaurant, as usual. They all felt sorry for me and Céleste told me, 'There's no one like a mother.' When I left they came to the door with me.

(Albert Camus, *The Outsider*)

Every sentence is separated from the next by a gap, which needs to be filled by the reader. Even in a passage as short as this, something goes on which is not told. What happened between the time the main character caught the bus and the time s/he arrived at the restaurant? What was hot? What happened during the meal? To whom does *they* refer? The ease or difficulty with which you are able to answer these questions depends on your mind's capacity to infer missing bits of information. And your capacity to infer relies, once again, on your world knowledge and contextual clues: you know, for example, what one usually does in a bus and in a restaurant. So, this knowledge helps you fill the gaps between one sentence and the next.

When you first read the extract above your inference skills were probably activated without your knowledge since you linked the four sentences automatically without thinking about it. In other cases, however, you may have to be more conscious of the gaps that need filling. Take the following sentence, for example:

Her right hand skimmed lightly the end of the table, and when she had passed on towards the sofa the carving knife had vanished without the slightest sound from the side of the dish.

(Joseph Conrad, *The Secret Agent*)

Here the gap (indicated by the comma) is very short, but crucial for the understanding of the scene, and it is not so easy to bridge it. What happens in the fraction of time when the woman walks to the sofa? How did the knife vanish? In this case you have to think a little harder, and your capacity to infer missing bits of information is more conscious.

In comics, because of the way texts are laid out, inferencing skills need to be active all the time. When reading comics, you need to form a whole out of all the bits and pieces of information that are laid out in every page. In Unit one of this book you read about the *gutter*, the white space that separates panels from each other. The presence of the gutter means that there is always a gap that needs to be filled by the readers every time they move from one panel to the next. The gutter can represent a gap in time or in space, or both.

Look at passages in Figure 3.7a and b. How different are the gutters in the two texts? How much and what kind of information do you have to infer in order to bridge the gaps between the panels? What are the effects of these two different narrative techniques?

Figure 3.7a

53

Figure 3.7b

The two passages are very different in the way the gutters are used. In Figure 3.7a the gaps between the panels are very short. The sequence of panels looks almost like a series of film frames. All the panels revolve around the same character and the same event – an elderly woman switching off the TV and preparing a sandwich. The scene is therefore very slow. This slowness reflects the slow movements of the woman. The large number of panels used to represent such a simple scene may also emphasise the fact that the only things that can be told about the old woman's life are such insignificant actions as the preparation of a sandwich. Panels that, in other cases, would seem unnecessary are used here to represent the tedious uneventfulness of the character's life.

Figure 3.7b is very different. The first four panels seem totally disconnected from one another. The scene is a completely different one in each panel and it is much harder to bridge the gaps between them and to make sense of what seems to be only a collection of panels put together at random. The fifth and final panel reveals the link: a worker in a photo lab has been developing different people's snaps. Perhaps you managed to guess, even before seeing the fifth panel, that this short text had something to do with the idea of significant occasions, but it takes a lot of inferencing skills and knowledge of particular cultural traditions even to get this far.

It is important to note that the use of adjectives like 'short', 'narrow', 'long' etc. for the description of gutters does not refer to the physical distance between the panels, but it refers to how closely related they are. Some authors of comics, for example, prefer to place panels attached to one another, without any space between them, but that doesn't mean that the gutter is not there or that it is less important. The gutter is a conceptual gap, not necessarily a physical one. For example, the gutters in Figure 3.7b are exaggeratedly wide in order to create a sense of puzzlement in the reader and, at the same time, to create a surprise effect with the final panel (which was shown overleaf in the original text).

Sometimes the story flows very smoothly, with many repeated elements indicating links among panels. This is typical of children's comics, for example, where reading should not normally require any extra effort. In such comics, the separation between the panels is minimised as much as possible and the gutter is only a blank, empty space between the panels, which readers can skip effortlessly. When there is a change of scene, normally there is also a caption which guides the readers in the right direction.

In comics for adults, instead, what is *not* told is just as important as what is told, and what is hidden is just as important as what is shown. The gutter is an essential part of the narrative, because it contains all the missing elements that the readers need to infer in order to reconstruct the story. As a result, readers cannot just 'jump over' the gutter, but they need to pause and think of possible ways to see 'inside' it.

In comics texts, therefore, cohesion and coherence have their own well-defined spaces: the former is found inside the panels and the latter in the gutter.

SUMMARY

Comics are made up of series of panels, and these are arranged so that between each panel and the next there is a white space called the gutter. This is a fundamental difference between comics and cartoons, which have only one single panel. This unit has looked at ways in which panels are linked to one another and at the role of the gutter. In making sense of strips of panels, readers rely both on explicit indications of links (cohesion), mainly in the form of repetition, and on their capacity to find other, more implicit connections, and infer whatever is missing from the narrative (coherence). The gutter is often a very important element in the narrative, because it represents the empty place that the reader needs to fill in order to reconstruct the story.

The voices of comics

AIM OF THIS UNIT

This unit will address the question of **voice**: who speaks in comics? You will also learn about the way in which speech and thought are represented and you will be able to make a comparison between 'conventional' literature and comics.

FICTIONAL VOICES: CAN YOU HEAR THEM?

The greatest part of fiction is made up of storytelling, and stories have characters. What the characters say to each other and, sometimes, what they think is very important in novels, short stories and, of course, comics, too. However these media are printed on paper, so the question is – how can the characters' speech and thought be represented in printed form? You are probably familiar with the use of quotation marks (single or double) to represent dialogues:

(a)   'Nice hat,' said the money-changer. 'Where did you get it?'
      'New York,' I told him.

                                     (Rehman Rashid, *A Malaysian Journey*)

Here it is very clear that there is a dialogue between two characters and you know exactly what they say to each other. This type of representation is called **direct speech** (DS), because the words spoken by the characters are reproduced *directly*, without the mediation of the **narrator** (more on the narrator later). But things aren't always this easy. What happens if the two lines above are changed?

> (b) The money-changer said that I had a nice hat, and asked me where I'd got it. I told him that I'd bought it in New York.

In this case you still clearly understand that a dialogue must be going on, but you don't know the *exact* words exchanged between the two characters. This type of representation is not as direct as in (a) above, because the words have been mediated by the narrator. Therefore it is called **indirect speech** (IS). So, in cases of indirect speech, dialogues are reported in the narrator's own words rather than in the character's.

Activity

To familiarise yourself with the concepts of DS and IS, transform passage 1 below into IS and passage 2 into DS. What changes do you need to make?

1   'I came down from Bangkok, and before that Hong Kong. I've been away a long time,' I said.
     'And now you've come home,' said Shafie.
     'Now I've come home.'
     'That's good. This is a good country.'
     'I know.'

2   I asked him what he did the rest of the time, and he said that he did other things like sitting at home and planting vegetables. He led a simple life.

(Note: there is a commentary on this activity on p. 97.)

WHO'S SPEAKING?

You have seen how IS involves a degree of manipulation of the actual words uttered by the characters. You have also learned that the person who changes the characters' words is called the narrator. It is important to understand that the narrator is not the author of the novel or short story, not a real person, but is as fictional as all the other characters. The following example will clarify the concept:

> My name is Karim Amir, and I am an Englishman born and bred, almost.

The extract above is the opening line of *The Buddha of Suburbia*, a novel written by Hanif Kureishi – not by Karim Amir, the narrator, who is of course only a fictional character in the story.

This means that the narrator's voice intermingles with the many other voices in the story. The only difference is that the narrator has a special role: it is the narrator who decides how to report the other characters' voices. Whenever you come across a piece of reported speech, then, the question is: who's speaking? Or, whose voice is it? The examples seen so far are quite straightforward, since with DS it is the characters' own voices, while with IS it is the narrator's voice.

But things can be more complicated than that. Consider the passage below:

> Mariam Binti Sharif was saying her prayers, but I was welcome to come in and wait for her. I was Rashid's son? Fancy that. My, how I had grown. Tok Yam would surely be happy to see me. Would I care for something to drink?
>
> (Rehman Rashid, *A Malaysian Journey*)

Who's speaking here? Is it the narrator? Maybe, but whose words are they? Whose voice is it? Answering these questions is not as easy as it was in the earlier examples. In fact, there seem to be two voices intertwined together. It is not pure DS nor is it IS. Sometimes the term **free indirect speech** is used to describe this type of reported speech. There is no need to go into great detail at this point. However, it is important to notice that, in certain cases, the narrator's voice becomes 'intrusive' and 'invades' the characters' speech, so that it is not always easy to separate the narrator's voice from the characters' voices.

THOUGHT PRESENTATION: READING THE CHARACTERS' MINDS

Superficially, the presentation of thought looks very similar to the presentation of speech. **Direct thought** (DT) is the equivalent of *direct speech*, and **indirect thought** (IT) corresponds to *indirect speech*:

(a) DT: 'It will be nice,' she thought.

(b) DS: 'It will be nice,' she said.

(c) IT: She thought that it would be nice.

(d) IS: She said it would be nice.

However, there is an important difference to consider. When the characters' speech is presented, especially in the direct mode, the reader will accept it without questioning whether or not the dialogue really took place in the story. But, when thought is presented, the reader has to accept much more: the fact that the narrator is able to see inside the characters' minds. In real life you may try to guess people's thoughts or feelings by looking at their facial expressions, gestures, behaviour etc., but can you be sure of their *precise* thoughts?

Also, can you be certain that people's thoughts may be expressed in words? What goes on in our minds is not necessarily always made up of language! So, thought presentation can be considered as more artificial than speech presentation, because it involves more 'interference' from the narrator.

This means that in the case of thought presentation it is never very clear who the voice belongs to: the character? the narrator? or both?

Activity

Read the following passage and pay attention to the way thought is reported. Whose words are those reported within quotation marks? Why?

'I am very old,' he thought sleepily. 'Every month I become a year more old. I was very young, and a fool to boot, when I took Mahbub's message to Umballa. Even when I was with that white Regiment I was very young and small and had no wisdom. But now I learn every day, and in three years the Colonel will take me out of the madrissah and let me go upon the Road with Mahbub hunting for horses' pedigrees, or maybe I shall go by myself; or maybe I shall find the lama and go with him. Yes; that is best. To walk again as a chela with my lama when he comes back to Benares.' The thoughts came more slowly and disconnectedly.

(Rudyard Kipling, *Kim*)

Commentary

This is a case of direct thought. However, unlike direct speech, direct thought doesn't necessarily represent the actual words thought by the character. You don't have to accept the fact that the narrator has access to the character's mind. In fact, it is probably easier to accept indirect thought than direct thought, as the former at least doesn't pretend to be a faithful report of thought. If you take into consideration examples (a) and (c) on p. 60, the latter could be interpreted as the narrator's guess: 'She seemed to think that it would be nice'; while the former implies the fact that the narrator *knows* the exact words inside the character's mind and therefore it is harder to believe and accept. For this reason, direct thought perhaps involves *more* interference from the narrator than does indirect thought. It is interesting that, in the passage above, the narrator says that 'the thoughts came more slowly and disconnectedly', as if to admit that what is reported is the narrator's own representation of the character's thoughts. In any case, however, it is notable that, once again, and even more than in reported speech, the voices of the characters and that of the narrator intermingle so much that it is sometimes difficult to separate one from the other.

Now that you have some understanding of the ways in which speech and thought are reported in literary texts like novels and short stories, you are ready to explore what happens in comics.

VOICES IN COMICS

The first thing to notice is that in comics speech and thought are only reported directly. Speech balloons and thought balloons are the equivalent of direct speech and direct thought respectively:

'Hmm . . . Who wrote it?'

is the same as

if it is DS, or

if it is DT. Every element of DS and DT has its equivalent in comics:

in literature	in comics
quotation marks	balloon border
DS introductory clause ('she said . . .')	balloon tail
DT introductory clause ('he thought . . .')	small bubbles

So, the presentation of speech and thought in comics may seem to be very straightforward and, in general, much simpler than it is in conventional literary texts. However, this is not always necessarily the case. What complicates things is, once again, the voice of the narrator.

If the voices in the balloons belong to the characters, the question is: how and where is the narrator's voice expressed in comics? In Unit one you learned that one of the main components of comics is the caption, and the *easy* answer to the question above is that the narrator's voice is 'heard' precisely in the caption. Sometimes captions only contain simple time references, like 'meanwhile . . .', 'the next day . . .', 'four years later . . .' and so on, which help the reader follow the time-line of the story. At other times captions carry much more information.

Figure 4.1 is a typical example in which the caption contains the story told by the narrator, while the remaining part of the panel shows characters speaking to each other by means of balloons.

Figure 4.1

Here the caption has a very similar function to the 'voice-over' that is sometimes used in films: that of providing extra information beyond the dialogues exchanged by the characters.

In the example seen so far the narrator's voice is entirely contained in the caption and, therefore, kept separate from the characters' voices. This seems to be quite different from conventional literature, where, as you saw earlier, the narrator's voice is much more intrusive and often merges with the characters' speech. Now the interesting thing is to find out whether or not this may happen in comics.

Activity

The panels in Figure 4.2 show one character's monologue. Despite the fact that no captions are present, can you 'hear' the narrator's voice at all? If so, write captions for each panel, changing the text as you think necessary.

(Note: there is a commentary on this activity on p. 98.)

Figure 4.2

THOUGHT BALLOONS

Earlier in the unit, thought presentation was described as a little artificial because it is difficult to imagine the fact that someone can 'read' someone else's mind (see p. 60). That observation applies to comics too. So the question is: can we trust thought balloons?

Activity

Look at the two panels in Figure 4.3. Can you understand what happens? Provide the words that you think the character may be thinking.

Figure 4.3

Commentary

You probably found it a little difficult to do this activity. The reason is that, without the words, there aren't many clues as to what is happening. Or, rather, the visual clues that *are* there don't actually help much in under-standing the scene. The thought balloons are then crucially important for the reader, since they provide the only clear indications of what is actually going on. So, once again, the function of these balloons seems to have more to do with informing the reader about the story than with what goes on inside the character's mind. The actual words in the balloons are:

panel 1:   *Jesus, is this guy following me or what?*

His actions are so unnatural.

panel 2:   *I'll test him. I'll stop and window-shop at this women's shoe store.*

These words give very precise clues about the actions shown in the panels. The thought balloon in the second panel is especially detailed, to the point of being unnatural. The action of stopping in front of the shop is something that must have happened in a split second, and the content of the balloon (two sentences) really seems far too long and elaborated. It really 'sounds' like the narrator's voice. In a caption, it would have been 'She stopped and window-shopped at a women's shoe store to test him.'

These last two activities have highlighted some important points about the presentation of speech and thought in comics:

- Despite their own well-defined spaces, the narrator's voice and the character's voices sometimes intermingle.

- This tends to happen in cases of monologues or reported thought, which have often the function of informing the reader about certain facts in the story.

- For this reason, monologues and the presentation of thought are virtually the same thing and are interchangeable.

In Figure 4.2 on p. 64, for example, the speech balloons could easily be transformed into thought balloons without causing any significant change. What really happens in this case is that the narrator speaks to the reader in the 'disguise' of a character's thoughts or monologue. This becomes even more evident when the character seems to be talking directly to the reader, as in Figure 4.4: is the character really speaking, or is the narrator making use of the speech balloon to address the reader?

Figure 4.4

Activity

To check your understanding of speech and thought presentation in comics and in conventional literature, look at the six panels in Figure 4.5 and produce a writing-only version of the text.

(Note: there is a commentary on this activity on p. 98.)

Figure 4.5

SUMMARY

Both in conventional literature and in comics the presentation of speech and thought is a very important element of storytelling. In general, both speech and thought can be reported by the narrator directly, with the 'real' words used by the characters, or indirectly, with the words partly changed by the narrator. In comics, the only mode of presentation of speech and thought is the direct one, by means of balloons. However, it can be seen that both in conventional literature and in comics the voice of the narrator sometimes 'invades' the space where the characters' voices are reported. This happens because the presentation of speech and thought is ultimately something artificial, which always requires the narrator's intervention, and the characters' voices can never be reported in a completely faithful manner.

The eyes of comics

AIM OF THIS UNIT

You know already that comics are a visual medium, and therefore *showing* and *seeing* are very important. This unit is all about showing and seeing and how these contribute to the construction of meaning in comics.

WHAT DOES 'POINT OF VIEW' MEAN?

Point of view has different meanings, all of which are common in everyday language:

◎　*visual* point of view is the literal sense, where 'view' means what is physically seen, e.g. 'from this point you can get a very nice view';

◎　*conceptual* point of view is the figurative sense and involves someone's opinion, rather than what they physically perceive, e.g. 'from my point of view the government has made a mistake';

◎　*interest* point of view does not involve perceiving or conceiving, but describes the position of someone or something with respect to a certain event, e.g. 'from the point of view of the tigers, the destruction of the forest is a huge problem'.

Although they are different, these three meanings are actually connected to one another, in the sense that the second and third meanings are derived from the first one, and in all three the concept of point of view is closely related to the ideas of position and *perspective*.

DEICTICS

In conventional narrative, point of view is important because, as readers mentally visualise the events narrated, they imagine themselves in a certain position in relation to other elements within each scene. The location of characters in space is rendered through **deictics**. Words like *here*, *there*, *this*, *that*, *up*, *down* and so on indicate the spatial position of the characters. For example, if you read the following sentence:

> The officious nurse came back.

you will probably imagine a situation in which a nurse must have left some time earlier and has now come back. *Back* where? Presumably to the place where someone else is located – the character whose point of view is being expressed. And you will 'see' the scene from this character's perspective. At this point the use of the attribute *officious* is interesting, since it clearly doesn't represent an objective description of the nurse, but must be the way the character sees her (or him). If the sentence had been written from the nurse's point of view, *came back* would probably be *went back*, while the attribute *officious* would probably not be there at all.

Comics are visual as well as verbal, and the angle from which characters, places and things are portrayed is very important. The visual perspective from which each panel is drawn carries a great deal of meaning.

Activity

What is the effect created by the point of view adopted in the panels in Figure 5.1? Could any other point of view generate the same effect? Think of other possibilities and describe how the effect would change.

Figure 5.1

Commentary

The first panel shows a character with a long road in front of him, which, together with the hills in the background and the ten-kilometre sign, contributes to conveying a sense of him being lost and helpless in that particular situation, apart from telling the readers that he has a long way to go. Probably a different point of view would not have had the same effect.

The second panel depicts two characters in a perspective that emphasises the distance between them. Again, this appears to be a deliberate choice: the physical distance reflects the emotional distance that separates the two. This, of course, is only one interpretation, and yours may be different, but what is important is that this interpretation is a result of precisely the point of view from which the panel is drawn.

When the perspective is vertical rather than horizontal, various effects can be generated. In the third panel, for example, a bottom-up point of view conveys a sense of threat.

When you read fiction, you know that what is told is not everything that took place in the story. If you read:

> Our second parting was final and irrevocable. The first time we had said goodbye, I thought we would never meet again. But I was mistaken.

you understand that two people must have met – at least twice – at different points in time. But you are not told what happened between the first meeting and the second. Narrative is very selective about what it chooses to tell. Because of this, there is always a difference between **story** and **plot**: the former refers to the actual chain of events (whether real or not) as they took place, and the latter refers to the way in which those events are told – *what* is told and *how* it is told.

So, the same story can be told from different points of view, producing very different results.

Activity

Figures 5.2 and 5.3 show two strips. Look at the first one and discuss and jot down ideas about the story:

◎   What is the main character doing?

◎   Who asks for the time?

◎   What is the relationship between the two characters?

◎   What is the main character thinking about in the last panel?

◎   What could be a possible title for this strip?

Now look at the second strip and see how far the notes you jotted down fit with this strip.

Now, considering both strips, try to answer the above questions again. What would be a possible title for the story?

(Note: there is a commentary on this activity on p. 99.)

Figure 5.2

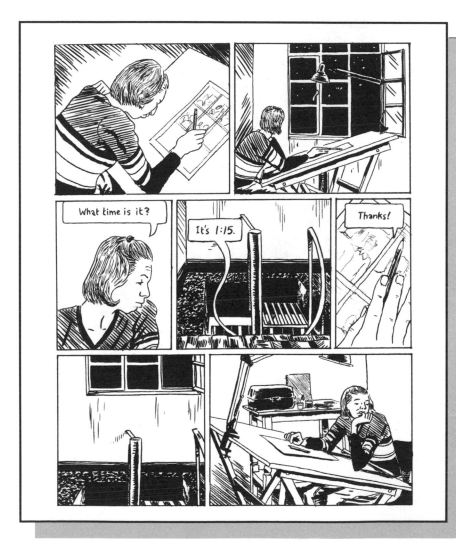

Figure 5.3

Activity

For each of the panels in Figure 5.4 write a short paragraph describing the scene in a narrative style. In doing so, focus your attention on these questions: Which personal pronouns would you use? Why? Is there a 'hero' in the scene?

Figure 5.4

Commentary

In the three panels, the reader views the characters from different perspectives. In (a), the two characters are in the same position in relation to the reader, and it is therefore difficult to decide who is the main character. The two are probably referred to simply as 'they'. In (b), only one character is shown. Here, however, it is unlikely that he might be seen as the 'hero' –

not so much because he's pointing a gun, but because he's pointing it right at the reader! In fact, he seems to be pointing the gun at the reader, but obviously there must be another character present in the same scene, who is the real target of the man. This other character is not shown because his point of view coincides completely with the reader's. The reader, that is, sees the scene through the character's eyes – this is an example of **internal point of view**. So, in this case, the identification between reader and character is virtually perfect, and it is natural to use the pronoun 'I' to refer to the character not seen in the panel, who, of course, is also the 'hero' of the story.

In (c), we understand that there are at least three characters, but only one of them is visible, while the presence of the other two is guessed because of the voices coming from nearby. Interestingly, only the back of the boy is shown, rather than the front. This means that what the reader sees is almost the same as what the boy sees. It's as if the reader is looking over the boy's shoulder. This near-coincidence of points of view helps generate a sense of identity between the reader and the character. In this case, then, the boy may be referred to as 'I', rather than 'him'.

The adoption of a certain vantage point and the ability to see things through the character's eyes are not the only ways in which the reader is drawn nearer to a character. Another common technique is the *close-up*, which is used extensively in film too, where the camera zooms in on the face of a character. Emphasis is on details of the facial expression, giving the reader hints about the character's feelings, emotions or mood.

Activity

Use the four stylised pairs of eyebrows (E1, E2, E3 and E4) and the four stylised mouths (M1, M2, M3 and M4) in Figure 5.5 to create simple faces that express the different emotions listed below (you can add more types of emotions, and more eyebrows and/or mouths, too). The first face is provided as an example. This activity is best carried out in two stages: the first stage, in which you create the faces, and a second stage, in which you compare your choices with those of other students, to see if there is any consensus on the ways eyebrows and mouths are combined together to symbolise the various expressions.

(Note: there is no commentary on this activity.)

Figure 5.5

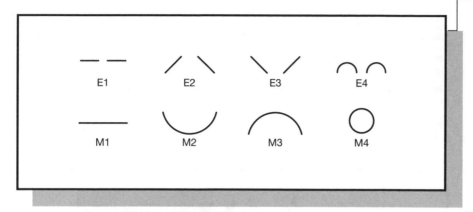

Example: annoyance

- ◎ anger
- ◎ happiness
- ◎ fear
- ◎ sadness
- ◎ joy
- ◎ seriousness
- ◎ surprise
- ◎ embarrassment
- ◎ disgust
- ◎ shyness.

Activity

Look at the series of four panels in Figure 5.6 and try to imagine what happens in the scene. What do you understand by looking at the two girls' faces? What are their emotions? What are they thinking? Why does the first girl (in the first, third and fourth panels) gradually change her expression? Discuss your interpretation with colleagues and compare it with theirs.

Figure 5.6

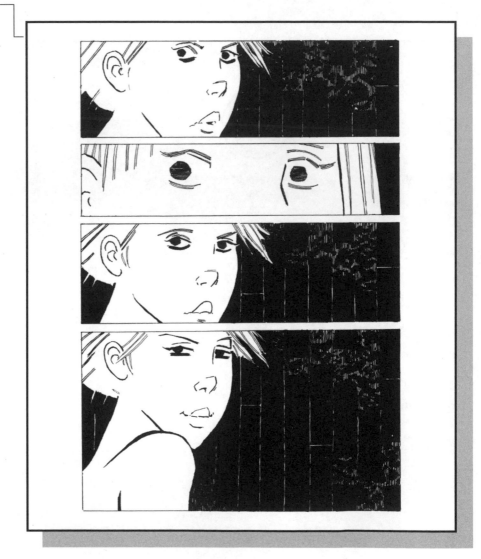

In the short sequence shown in Figure 5.6 the focus is on the two girls' faces. In a person's facial expression, the eyebrows, eyes and mouth are very important indicators of the person's emotions. In the first panel, the girl's eyebrows are sloping downwards (especially her left one), the eyes are wide open and the mouth is slightly open. Her emotion seems to be a mixture of surprise, indicated by her eyes and her mouth, and annoyance, indicated by her eyebrows. In the second panel, the mouth is not shown, but the eyes and the raised left eyebrow (the right one is not visible) of the other girl seem to express surprise and fear. In the third panel, the expression of the first girl seems to have mellowed slightly, as is indicated by the eyes, which are now not as wide open as earlier, and the right eyebrow, which is sloping upwards. In the fourth panel yet another change of expression occurs. The girl is now looking almost amused. Her eyelids are much lower and, importantly, the edges of her mouth are curved upwards, which is the typical sign of a smile. Her eyebrows are sloping downwards, however, and that produces a kind of condescending and slightly mocking expression on the girl's face.

Close-ups allow details of facial expressions to be shown and, thanks to that, the readers of a story can guess the character's feelings and emotions. In a way, it's as if they can gain some access into the character's mind (see also Unit four).

The point of view each panel is drawn from can allow even more direct access into the character's mind. You have already seen some panels where the reader sees the scene through the character's eyes. In these cases, however, you can't always be sure that what you see is indeed what the character sees, or even exactly *whose* point of view it is that is being followed. Consider, for example, the three panels in Figure 5.7 – Mrs Hicks is showing Leonard around the area, when they finally get to the town of Hicksville.

Is the third panel exactly what appears in front of the two characters? Probably it is, but we can't be absolutely certain.

There are some cases in which what is shown in the panel is so subjective that notions of 'reality' become almost irrelevant. This happens, for example, when a panel portrays a scene from a character's dream, imagination or fantasy life.

Figure 5.7

Put the nine panels in Figure 5.8 in what you think may be the right order and justify your choice. Be aware that these panels include a possible dream sequence, so this activity might be harder than you first think. (Note: the answer to this activity is on p. 100.)

Figure 5.8

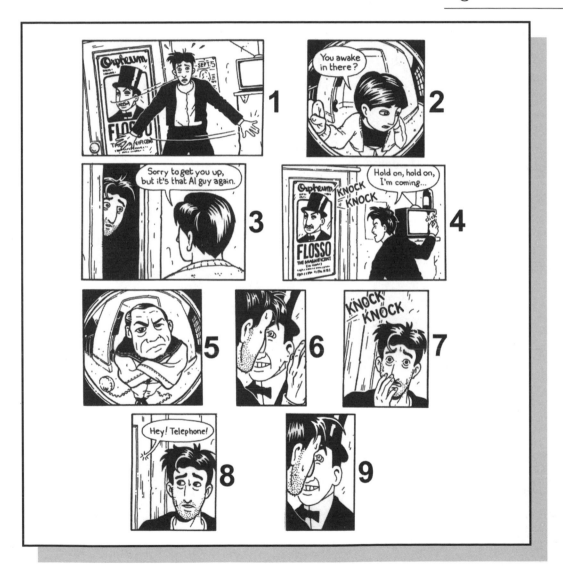

SUMMARY

As you learned in the first two units of this book, comics are both visual and verbal. This means that each page of a comic book is viewed as well as read. As a consequence, the point of *view* from which each individual panel is drawn is a major aspect of the way in which meaning is conveyed in comics. It is important at several levels:

◎   it contributes to creating various effects, such as closeness, distance, threat, subjectivity, objectivity etc.;

◎   it defines the positions of the characters within the story, and that of the reader in relation to the scenes narrated;

◎   it contributes to the identification of the reader with the main character;

◎   it helps the reader gain access to the characters' emotions and feelings and, sometimes, to their dreams, visions and imaginary thoughts.

Comics and computers

In this unit you are going to explore the relationship between comics and computers. In particular, the focus will be on how computers make use of some of the features of comics. In addition, the unit hints at ways in which comics may take advantage of the sophisticated graphic capabilities of computers.

COMICS IN COMPUTERS?

The word *computer* comes from the Latin verb *computare*, which means 'to calculate'. Indeed, computers were originally created and used in order to carry out complex calculations in a relatively short time. And when the first personal computers began to appear towards the end of the 1970s, their primary tasks still mainly involved numerical operations.

Over the years, however, computers have become much more versatile and capable of performing a much wider range of tasks. One of the most dramatic improvements has been in the way computers render graphics.

So, what has this to do with comics?

85

The relationship between comics and computers is an interesting one. The improved graphical capabilities of computers have had a major positive impact on virtually all aspects of computer applications, including their ease of use. Three areas, in particular, are closely related to comics:

◎ the Graphical User Interface (GUI);

◎ word processing;

◎ image creation and manipulation.

CARTOONS ON YOUR DESKTOP?

Years ago a computer screen would have looked like the one in Figure 6.1.

Figure 6.1

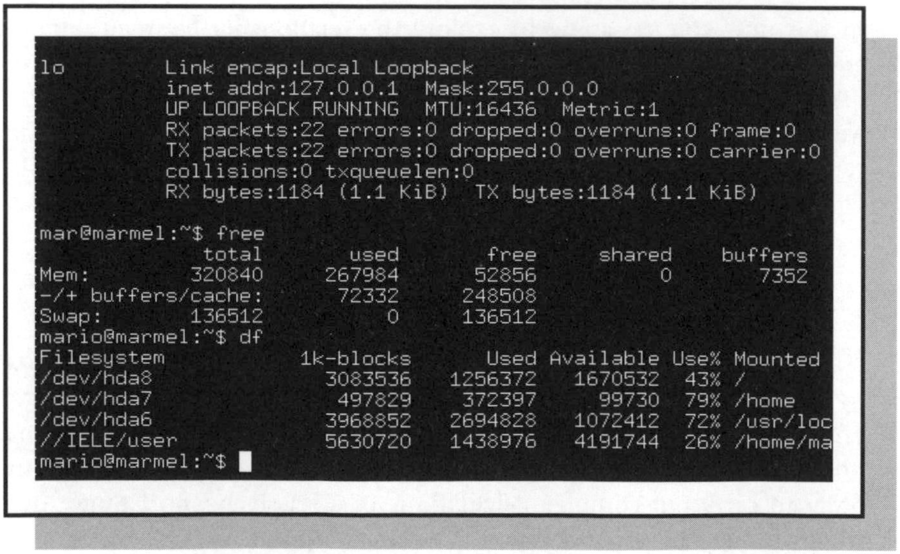

The idea of user-friendliness had yet to be invented! Nowadays, fortunately, things have improved a great deal and computers look much less threatening than they used to a couple of decades ago. In fact, over the years computers have developed enormously, not only in terms of what they can *do*, but also, and just as dramatically, in terms of *how easily* they can do it. Figure 6.2 shows a 'shot' of a modern computer screen.

Figure 6.2

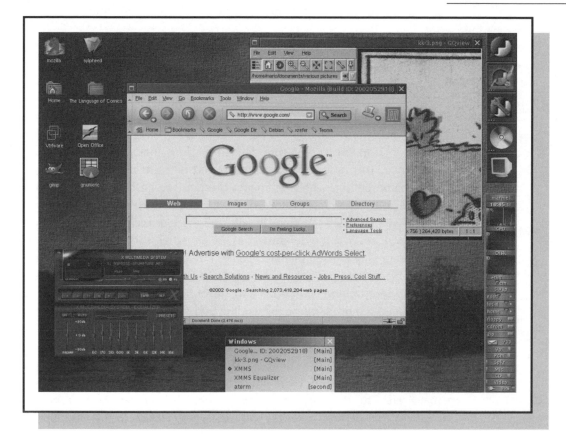

This is completely different, of course, from the dreary text-only display shown in the first image above. Computers have become more pleasing to the eye, more attractive and, above all, easier to understand. Developers have brought computers closer to the general public by gradually orienting their appearance towards things that people are familiar with. There has been a move from a series of arcane commands, very difficult for non-specialists to remember, to items which have the names and, to some extent, the looks of everyday objects, such as desktops, folders, documents and so on. The type of resemblance that exists between computer objects and real-life objects is particularly interesting here.

Look at Figure 6.2 on the previous page. You may not have seen some of the desktop icons before, but can you guess what types of programmes they are associated with? In doing this activity you may find it helpful to refer back to the section 'Semiotics and the idea of the sign', in Unit two.

This is a rather cluttered desktop, but is not an untypical one, as *multi-tasking* is a standard feature of modern computers. Essentially there are *icons* and *windows*. In Unit two, *icons* were defined as signs that create meaning by resemblance. This is a semiotic definition and different from how the term is used in computing, where all images used on the desktop of a computer are called *icons*, regardless of how they work. It is interesting to see whether, and how well, our desktop icons fit with the more academic definition. One thing to notice is that the desktop icons are all rather 'cartoony', in the sense that they are very stylised pictures. Some, however, seem to resemble iden-tifiable objects fairly clearly. The one labelled 'Sylpheed', for example, represents an envelope with a pen and, accordingly, you may have guessed that Sylpheed is a programme for sending and receiving e-mails. In this case, therefore, the desktop icon corresponds with the semiotic definition of icon given in Unit two.

An interesting icon is 'gimp'. It shows an animal, possibly a fox, with a paintbrush in its mouth. Here, although we may not be sure what the fox actually refers to, the presence of the paintbrush indicates the presence of something else, perhaps a canvas and some colour tubes. In this case, there-fore, the icon (associated with a programme of image creation and manipulation) seems to fit the semiotic definition of *index* better than it does that of *icon*.

'VMware' is harder to understand. It is virtually impossible to guess what the three squares refer to without knowing what the programme VMware actually does. Consequently, this icon is really a *symbol*, rather than an icon proper.

Below are the programmes associated with the rest of the desktop icons in Figure 6.2 – you can decide for yourself whether they're icons, indexes or symbols:

88

◎   'Mozilla' – indicates an Internet browser (Mozilla was the nickname of one of the most popular and earliest Internet browsers);

◎   'Open Office' – indicates an office 'suite' ('open' refers to the fact that anyone is free to modify the programme, if they wish or need to);

◎   'Gnumeric' – indicates a spreadsheet application.

Extension

Consider again the screen-shot in Figure 6.2 and identify all the elements that are commonly found in everyday life: what do they mean in a computer environment?

Commentary

Computer imagery makes extensive use of familiar objects. One that occurs very frequently is the picture of a house, often associated with the concept of 'home'. In the screen-shot there are three such images: one within a folder icon, another one in the 'toolbar' of an application, and a third as one of the 'shortcuts' in the Internet browser in the middle of the screen. In the first two cases 'home' refers to the folder in which users store their personal files; in the third case it refers to the first web page that the browser opens when it is started.

   Other objects include magnifying lenses, representing 'zoom' actions; spanners, which are normally associated with configuration tools; and a drawing-board pin, which indicates the possibility of sticking a window to the desktop. Also interesting is the graphical interface of the music player on the bottom-left part of the screen: the symbols used on the keys are exactly the same as those found on a real CD player, so that users know exactly how to use it, even the first time, without having to learn strange commands.

Familiarity, then, has been a primary objective for computer developers. Cartoon-like images used as desktop icons or as buttons on toolbars and menu-bars have the objective of making the interface easy to understand and to remember. But the similarity between computers' GUIs and comics doesn't end here.

Interactivity is another important feature of modern computers, which are increasingly capable of communicating with people. While people tap on keyboards, click on mouse buttons, or even speak to computers, these don't simply run programmes, but also reply to their human users, and they do it in a way that is direct, easy and, again, reassuringly familiar and friendly. And what is more direct, easier, more familiar and friendlier than comics? With the same aim of facilitating their use, computer programmes often employ 'help balloons', which give various tips to the users as they perform certain tasks. Help balloons come directly from the language of comics, and can be considered computerised versions of speech and thought balloons. Figure 6.3 shows some examples.

Figure 6.3

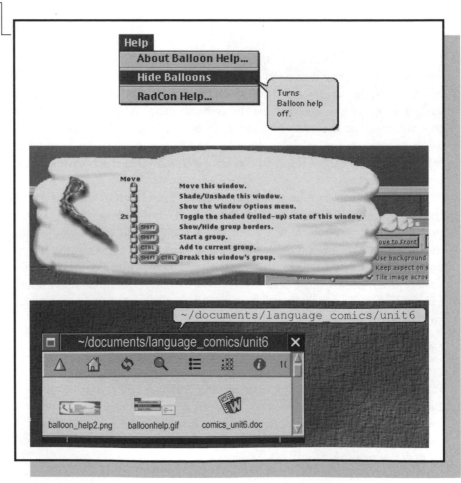

Some 'characters' have even becomes famous (or notorious?) (see Figure 6.4):

Figure 6.4

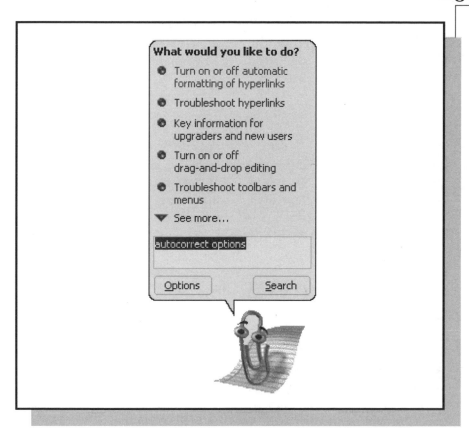

This cute (and often irritating) paper clip interacts with users through a speech balloon. Unlike conventional ones, however, this particular balloon is used both by the character and by his/her inter-locutors, who type their questions directly in the balloon itself.

WORDS AND COMICS

The talking paper clip is part of a popular word-processing package. Writing, too, is one of those areas that has benefited from the improved graphical rendering offered by modern computers. More and more people use computers to write all kinds of texts, such as letters, memos, articles, recipes and books like this one. Only a little longer than a decade ago, computer writing looked pretty much like typewriting, if not worse! Printers were not very sophisticated and computer screens only showed rather basic characters, like this:

```
This is what text looked like on computer screens
fifteen years ago.
```

Nowadays, thanks to much better graphics, and to the concept of WYSIWYG (What You See Is What You Get), text can be displayed and printed in many different styles (fonts), sizes (from two points to anything that the size of the page/screen allows), colours (up to sixteen million), effects (embossed, engraved, outlined etc.) and orientation (upwards, downwards etc.):

We **now** HAVE an incredible range **of** creative *possibilities!*

Text, therefore, can be treated graphically and, when it is, letters and words become images. As a consequence, the meaning potential of the written word multiplies by as many times as our creativity allows it to grow. You have already learned about the importance of the pictorial aspect of writing in Unit two. With the help of computers it can really be exploited almost endlessly. To explore the role of graphological effects in a range of different texts, see the core book in this series, *Working with Texts*, and also the satellite title *The Language of Advertising*.

Another thing that has become much easier now is the ability to insert pictures into texts. Any type of image can be included, such as one that you have drawn yourself, a photograph that you have previously scanned, an image that you have downloaded from the Internet, a *clipart* image, or even a screen-shot of your computer desktop! This can be of great help in descriptive and explanatory texts, where the possibility to show objects and places referred to is of fundamental importance.

(Note: this activity and the next two should be conducted in succession.)

Using word-processing software, write a short promotional leaflet for an aspect of your school/college provision. Incorporate some photographs into the text (scanned in, or perhaps downloaded from the school/college web site) to aid your description. Then explain the way in which the pictures relate to the text.

You will probably find that the pictures you have used illustrate the text, in the sense that they show some of the activities and people that you think are important. Their function is therefore similar to that of the photographs that accompany newspaper articles.

Scanners are not always available, and downloading images may be too time consuming and unreliable. For this reason, all major word-processing packages always include interesting alternatives in the set of so-called *clipart galleries*. These images are ready-made, highly stylised pictures that represent a wide range of situations, places, objects and people.

Use the same text as in the previous activity but this time use clipart images to illustrate your material. How does the relationship between text and pictures change, compared to the previous activity? What difficulties did you find in choosing the images?

Here you can't expect the pictures to illustrate your text in the same way as the photographs did earlier. The clipart images don't show real places, things or people, but only *represent* them. This means that both you and your readers have to work a little harder to find the links between words and pictures. It also confirms that stylised pictures are often harder to deal with than photographs or very realistic images.

Now really put your creativity to the test. Using only pictures from the clipart galleries available on your computer, create a humorous four-panel comic strip.

(Note: there are no commentaries on these activities.)

ARTISTS WITH MICE

Another area that has improved greatly over the years is that of graphical applications, which can be used to create or manipulate images in very sophisticated ways. A new breed of artists is emerging – artists who don't use brushes and canvases but mice and computer screens. However, even without possessing a great artistic talent, everyone can try out some of the possibilities offered by such programmes. The easiest things to experiment with are graphic filters and distortion tools. A simple clipart image can be transformed into many different versions (see Figure 6.5).

Figure 6.5

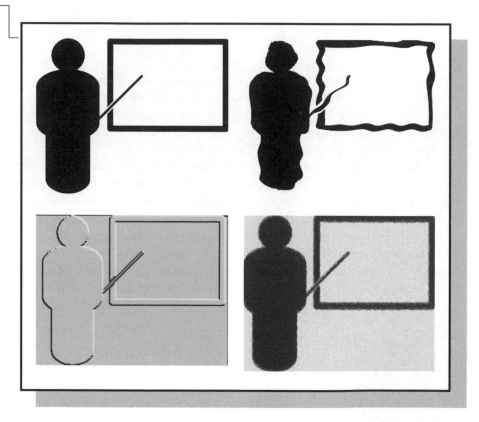

Each different version conveys a different effect, according to how it is interpreted.

Activity

Use the strip you created in the previous activity and make different versions of it by applying some of the graphic filters and distortion tools available in your favourite graphics software. How has the strip changed? What effects do the various versions of the strip convey now? You can do the same activity with a real comic strip, which you can either scan or download from the Internet.

(Note: there is no commentary on this activity.)

SUMMARY

Comics were first created more than a century ago and, since then, have always been based on very simple tools – paper, pencil and, optionally, colours. Computers, on the other hand, are much more recent products, based on very complex technology, which becomes more and more advanced as time passes. However, as you have seen in this unit, between comics and computers there are some interesting points of contact. Computers make use of the imagery and of some of the conventions of the language of comics and, at the same time, comics can benefit from the immense possibilities offered by computer graphics. This latter aspect is still under-explored but will no doubt yield very interesting results in the years to come.

answers and commentaries

Unit four, p. 58

To transform DS into IS is not just a matter of removing the quotation marks: you have to make certain other changes too. You won't need to go into the technical details of this here, but what is important is that you understand the basic difference between these two types of reported speech: in DS dialogues are reported faithfully, while in IS they are somewhat manipulated by the narrator. So, passage 1 could be changed into:

> I said that I had come down from Hong Kong and Bangkok and that I had been away a long time. Shafie asked me whether I had come home now, and I said that I had. He said that Malaysia was a good country, and I told him that I knew it.

In this case there are changes in tenses (past simple to past perfect), the introduction of some phrases like 'I said that ...', 'He said that ...' and 'Shafie asked me whether ...', and the transformation of a pronoun into a noun ('this' has become 'Malaysia'). These are typical examples of manipulation that are made to dialogues when they are reported in IS. Passage 2 could be rewritten as:

> 'What do you do the rest of the time?' I asked him.
>   'Other things. Sit at home. Plant vegetables. A simple life,' he replied.

In this case the dialogue is represented so that the words match those actually used by the characters.

You can find further work on this area in Intertext's *The Language of Fiction*.

Unit four, p. 64

In this comics page a character (who is also the protagonist in the story) is apparently talking to himself. In drama this type of speech is called mono-logue. In real life people do talk to themselves sometimes, in what is generally called 'thinking aloud'. But the two – thinking aloud and monologue – are not exactly the same. People often talk to themselves because hearing their own voice helps them understand something better. The speech produced on these occasions is not necessarily well formed, complete or even coherent. More commonly it is fragmentary, disconnected and not very long. In drama, on the other hand, monologues are normally well formed and coherent stretches of speech, which can sometimes go on for a considerable length of time! This is because monologues in drama have a fundamentally different function. They are used to provide the audience with some important elements of the story that would be difficult or perhaps stylistically clumsy to give otherwise. A character who speaks on stage to no other characters seems to be thinking aloud but actually speaks to the audience. The char-acter, in such cases, takes up the role of the narrator. It's as if the narrator uses the character's voice to speak directly to the audience. And this is precisely what happens in Figure 4.2. Toge, the protagonist in the book, seems to be reflecting on the events that have occurred recently. Perhaps he *is* reflecting, but the main function of this monologue is to give the readers time references ('for a whole year', 'in the past six months') and to inform them about some key elements in the story (the secret documents are hidden somewhere in rubbish pit). The narrator's voice, then, is intruding into Toge's speech balloons.

This activity should have made you realise that the presentation of speech in comics is not as simple as it seems to be at first.

Unit four, p. 68

Here you have various possibilities. You can decide to keep as close to the original as possible, maintaining all the speech in the direct mode:

> I was driving my truck when I saw some cars ahead in the middle of the road. There had been an accident. A girl was lying on the ground hurt.
> 'Hold on love. It won't be long,' I said as I walked towards her.
> 'How do you feel?' I asked, as I realised that she had a broken leg.
> 'Has someone called an ambulance?' I asked her mother.
> 'Yes,' she replied. 'Will she be alright?'
> 'I really don't know,' I admitted.

'You are a doctor, aren't you?'

'Nah, I'm a forklift driver.'

'Shouldn't you keep away?' she asked, worried.

Or you can use the indirect mode:

I was driving my truck when I saw some cars ahead in the middle of the road. There had been an accident. A girl was lying on the ground, hurt. As I walked towards her I reassured her that it wouldn't be long before she got some help. I realised that she had a broken leg and asked her mother whether an ambulance had been called. She said that it had, and wanted to know if the girl would be alright; I told her that I didn't know. At that point she asked me if I was a doctor, but I informed her that I was only a forklift driver. At that point she became more worried, and said that maybe I should keep away.

Or you could even make the passage much shorter:

As I was driving, I saw an accident. A girl was hurt and I tried to help. The mother didn't seem reassured when I told her that I was only a forklift driver.

Of course many more options are possible. The main difference between these three versions is the different role of the narrator. From the first to the third the narrator is increasingly in control, as the character's voices are gradually replaced by the narrator's voice.

Unit five, p. 75

The two strips are about the same story, in the sense that they narrate events which took place at the same time, in the same house, involving the same people. However, the two strips have a different plot. What happens may be the same, but what is shown is not. The first strip is drawn from the woman's perspective, while the second follows the man's, resulting in two totally different strips. That confirms the fact that the plot is always selective: choices are made about which character(s) to portray, which places, which events and, of course, from which (or whose) point of view. Such choices imply that a great deal of the story is actually left out of the plot. One consequence of this is that, as you saw in Unit three, readers have to reconstruct the story by filling the gaps.

Another important consequence has to do with deictics. The physical location of the characters within each panel is a crucial indicator for the reader to understand who the main characters are, and whose point of view is followed. In the first strip the woman is much closer to the reader, and the man is not even shown, while his voice is 'heard' coming from downstairs. In the second strip the exact opposite applies: the woman is not shown, and her voice comes from upstairs (notice the deictic value of words like *downstairs* and *upstairs*). The position of the characters in relation to the reader is sometimes called the *vantage position*, which is very important for the process of identification of the reader with the 'hero'.

Unit five, p. 83

The reconstruction of the right sequence depends on how you interpret point of view. Here, there seems to be an event that happens twice – someone knocks on the door and the main character (Ernie) looks through the peephole to check who it is. In one panel the peephole shows the image of a woman (Marie), and in another panel it shows a man with a ball chained to his foot (Howard, Ernie's deceased brother). Ernie looks visibly shocked in at least two panels, probably as a reaction of what he saw. The question, then, is: who is really behind the door? In panel 3 Ernie opens the door and the reader sees that the one who was knocking is Marie. That Marie is a real person is confirmed by the fact that the panel is drawn from an **external point of view**, and both Ernie and Marie are shown. Consequently, the appearance of Howard must be the result of a kind of hallucination Ernie suffered from for a moment. If this is the case, panel 5 (i.e. panel 3 in the correct version on the previous page) shows *exactly* what Ernie sees and represents an insight into his mind.

CHESTER COLLEGE WARRINGTON LIBRARY

references and further reading

REFERENCES

Comics

Campbell, Eddie (2000) *Alec: The King Canute Crowd*. Paddington, NSW: Eddie Campbell Comics.

Clowes, Daniel (1998) *Ghost World*. Seattle, Wash.: Fantagraphics Books.

Hart, Tom (1998) *The Sands*. Montreal: Black Eye Books.

Horrocks, Dylan (1998) *Hicksville*. Montreal: Black Eye Books.

Kanan, N. (1999) *Lost Girl*. New York: NBM.

Kuper, Peter (1996) *Eye of the Beholder*. New York: NBM.

Kuper, Peter (1997) *The System*. New York: DC Comics.

Kuper, Peter (2000) *Topsy Turvy*. New York: Eye Press.

Lutes, Jason (1997) *Jar of Fools*. Montreal: Black Eye Books.

Madden, Matt (n.d.) 'Exercises in style', *Indy Magazine*, available at <http://www.indymagazine.com/comics/style.shtml>. Last accessed 18 December 2002.

Moore, Alan and Campbell, Eddie (1999) *From Hell*. Paddington, NSW: Eddie Campbell Comics.

Seth (1996) *It's a Good Life If You Don't Weaken*. Montreal: Drawn and Quarterly.

Tezuka, Osamu (1995) *Adolf: A Tale of the Twentieth Century*. San Francisco, Calif.: Cadence Books.

Tezuka, Osamu (1996) *Adolf: An Exile in Japan*. San Francisco, Calif.: Cadence Books.

Tomine, Adrian (1995) *32 Stories*. Montreal: Drawn and Quarterly.

Tomine, Adrian (1998) *Sleepwalk and Other Stories*. Montreal: Drawn and Quarterly.

Tommaso, Richard (1995) *Clover Honey*. Seattle, Wash.: Fantagraphics Books.

Watson, Andi (2001) *Breakfast After Noon*. Portland, Oreg.: Oni Press.

Literary texts

Camus, A. (1982) *The Outsider*. London: Hamish Hamilton.

Conrad, J. (2000) *The Secret Agent*. London: Penguin.

Kipling, R. (2000) *Kim*. London: Penguin.

Kureishi, H. (1990) *The Buddha of Suburbia*. London: Faber & Faber.

Rashid, R. (1993) *A Malaysian Journey*. Petaling Jaya (self-published by the author).

FURTHER READING

Baetens, J. (ed.) (2001) *The Graphic Novel*. Leuven: Leuven University Press.

Barker, M. (1984) *A Haunt of Fears: The Strange History of the British Horror Comics Campaign*. London: Pluto Press.

Barker, M. (1989) *Comics: Ideology, Power and the Critics*. Manchester: Manchester University Press.

Chandler, Daniel (2001) *Semiotics: The Basics*. London: Routledge.

Eisner, W. (1985) *Comics and Sequential Art*. Tamarac, Fla.: Poorhouse Press.

Eisner, W. (1995) *Graphic Storytelling*. Tamarac, Fla.: Poorhouse Press.

Fiske, J. (1990) *Introduction to Communication Studies*. London: Routledge.

Goodman, S. (1996) 'Visual English', in S. Goodman and D. Graddol (eds), *Redesigning English*. London: Routledge, pp. 38–72.

Harvey, R. C. (1994) *The Art of the Funnies*. Jackson, Miss.: University Press of Mississippi.

Harvey, R. C. (1996) *The Art of the Comic Book*. Jackson, Miss.: University Press of Mississippi.

Kress, G. and van Leeuwen, T. (1996) *Reading Images: The Grammar of Visual Design*. London: Routledge.

McCloud, S. (1994) *Understanding Comics: The Invisible Art.* New York: HarperCollins.

McCloud, S. (2000) *Reinventing Comics.* New York: DC Comics.

Sabin, R. (1993) *Adult Comics: An Introduction.* London: Routledge.

Sabin, R. (1996) *Comics, Comix and Graphic Novels.* London: Phaidon Press.

index of terms

coherence   45

A sentence or a text is coherent when the ideas it contains make consistent sense to the hearer/reader. Unlike **cohesion**, coherence is based on subjective judgements.

cohesion   36

The patterns of language created within a text, mainly within and across sentence boundaries, and which collectively make up the organisation of larger units of the text such as paragraphs. Cohesion can be both lexical and grammatical. Lexical cohesion is established by means of chains of words of related meaning linking across sentences; grammatical cohesion is established mainly by grammatical words such as 'the' 'this', 'it' and so on.

content words   5

Words which refer to things, people, states, ideas etc. The vast majority of words, in any language, are of this type. Content words are generally considered in opposition to **functional words**. The set of content words is subject to continuous change, as new words appear, some fall into disuse and the meaning of some others vary with time.

deictics   72

Deictics are words which point backwards, forwards and extra-textually and which serve to situate a speaker or writer in relation to what is said. For example, in the sentence, 'I'm going to get some wine from that shop over there', the main deictic words are 'that' and 'there'.

direct speech   58

A way of reporting speech in narrative, in which the words spoken by the characters are reproduced *directly*, without the mediation of the **narrator**. For example: 'The food is excellent!' he said. See also **indirect speech**.

direct thought   60

A way of reporting thought in narrative, in which the words 'thought' by the characters are reproduced *directly*, without the mediation of the **narrator**. For example: 'I have to rush home,' he thought. Because it entails the ability to 'read' the characters' minds, this form of reported thought is considered a more artificial narrative convention than **indirect thought**.

external point of view   101

It indicates that a particular scene, or a larger portion of the story, is narrated from a perspective external to any of the characters. Whether this is the case it is not always easy to establish. A description of a place without any character being present, for example, would be one of the few clear cases of external point of view. (See also **internal point of view** and **point of view**.)

extra-textual context 36

In general, anything that, physically or metaphorically, surrounds a text. The extra-textual context includes the physical environment where the text is situated, the reader's world knowledge, and also other texts that are somehow relevant to the particular text in question.

free indirect speech 59

A way of reporting speech in narrative, in which the words spoken by the characters are reproduced *indirectly* by the **narrator**, while no indication is given of the fact that it is indeed reported speech. For example: Was the food too hot? She always wanted to make sure I was comfortable. See also **indirect speech**.

functional words 5

Words which do *not* refer to things, people, states or ideas, but are used to syntactically link **content words** together. Functional words include articles, prepositions, conjunctions and pronouns. Also, unlike content words, the set of functional words tends to remain unchanged in time (changes occur over very long periods, if at all).

given information 38

Any information, in a sentence, which was already mentioned earlier in a previous sentence. The concept 'given information' is generally considered, and best understood, in conjunction with the concept **new information**.

gutter 9

The blank space that separates each **panel** from the others. The gutter is similar to the space that divides one sentence from the next: there is always a certain amount of information that is missing from the narrative, and the readers have to provide it by themselves.

icon 15

A **sign** whose meaning is based on a resemblance between one aspect of the sign itself and what the sign refers to. For example, a picture of a cat, especially if realistically drawn, is an icon because it is visually similar to the cat it represents; the **onomatopoeic word** 'miaow' is an icon because its sound is similar to the noise made by cats. (See also **symbol** and **index**.)

index 15

A **sign** is an index when it indicates the presence of something else. Smoke, for example, is an index of fire. Smoke stands for fire, because it indicates its presence.

indirect speech 58

A way of reporting speech in narrative, in which the words spoken by the characters are reproduced *indirectly* by the **narrator**. For example: He said that the food was excellent. See also **direct speech**.

indirect thought 60

A way of reporting thought in narrative, in which the words 'thought' by the characters are reproduced *indirectly* by the **narrator**. For example: He felt that he had to rush home. Unlike

direct thought, this form of reported thought does not necessarily entail the ability to 'read' the characters' minds.

inference 46
The capacity to understand things indirectly, usually on the basis of incomplete information.

internal point of view 78
This indicates that a particular scene, or a larger portion of the story, is narrated through the perception of one of the characters. Whether this is the case is not always easy to establish. A subjective description of a place with a first-person **narrator** would be one of the few clear cases of internal point of view. (See also **external point of view** and **point of view**.)

narrator 58
The implied teller of a story or presenter of a text. It is important to remember that the narrator is in most cases distinct from the author of the text. Normally there can be a third-person narrator (not a participant in the story) or a first-person narrator (a participant in the story).

new information 38
Any information, in a sentence, which was not mentioned earlier in the text. The concept new information is generally considered, and best understood, in conjunction with the concept **given information**.

onomatopoeic words 7
Words whose sounds resemble noises associated with the things, animals or actions the words refer to. For example, 'crack', 'bang',

'miaow' and 'gulp' are all onomatopoeic words.

panel 7
A rectangular frame that contains pictures and, usually, **speech balloons** depicting a single scene within a narrative in comics. Each page of a comic book normally has six panels, separated by the **gutter**.

plot 74
The way in which a **story** is narrated. The plot is always selective, in that only certain events of the story are actually told, and sometimes not even in the right order.

point of view 71
In narrative, the perspective from which one or more scenes, or even the entire **story**, is narrated. Point of view is one of the most important aspect of the **plot**. It is distinct from **voice**.

semantic field 46
A group of words that are related in meaning, normally as a result of being connected with a particular context of use. For example, 'chop', 'simmer', 'boil' and 'herbs' are all connected with the semantic field of cookery.

semiotics 14
The study of both human and non-human communication, focusing on **signs** and sign systems (codes) and how they generate meaning.

sign 15
In **semiotics**, the term 'sign' is used with the widest meaning of 'something that has significance'. Signs are generally classified into **icons**, **indexes** and **symbols**.

speech balloon 9
> In comics, a bubble-like shape that contains the words spoken by characters. It is the equivalent of **direct speech** in narrative.

story 74
> In narrative, the actual series of events that 'took place' and constitute the base for a **plot**.

symbol 15
> A **sign** whose meaning is based on a shared convention. Words are typical examples of symbols. The sequence of letters 'd-o-g' stands for the idea of 'dog', not because it resembles a dog in any way, but because that is its conventional meaning in the English language. Similarly, the meanings of the colours red, orange and green are based on a shared convention. In these cases we also talk about arbitrary meaning. (See also **icon** and **index**.)

synonymy 43
> A type of relation between two or more words that occurs when the meanings of these words are very similar (complete equivalence is extremely rare). For example, the words 'enormous', 'huge', 'gigantic', 'massive' and 'colossal' are all synonyms (although you wouldn't always use them interchangeably).

textual context 36
> The textual environment within which each expression is situated. It is of fundamental importance for the comprehension of words, sentences or larger units of text.

thought balloon 9
> In comics, a cloud-like shape that contains the words thought by characters. It is the equivalent of **direct thought** in narrative.

voice 57
> In narrative, it indicates the person who speaks in any given scene of a story. The narrator is not necessarily the only voice in the plot, but the characters' voices may at times be 'heard', not only in **direct speech**, but also in ways that are not entirely predictable. Voice should not be confused with **point of view**.

ROUTLEDGE STUDY GUIDES

WORK SMARTER, NOT HARDER!

It's a simple fact - everyone needs a bit of help with their studies. Whether you are studying for academic qualifications (from A-levels to doctorates), undertaking a professional development course or just require good, common sense advice on how to write an essay or put together a coherent and effective report or project, Routledge Study Guides can help you realise your full potential.

Our impressive range of titles covers the following areas:

- Speaking
- Study Technique
- Thinking
- Writing

- Science
- English
- History
- Mathematics
- Politics

- Doctorate
- MBA
- Research

Available at all good bookshops or you can visit the website to browse and buy Routledge Study Guides online at:

www.study-guides.com
www.study-guides.com
www.study-guides.com
www.study-guides.com
www.study-guides.com

ROUTLEDGE